THE ECONOMICS OF MASS MIGRATION IN THE TWENTIETH CENTURY

The Washington Institute for Values in Public Policy is an independent, nonprofit research and educational organization that provides nonpartisan analyses exploring the ethical values underlying public policy issues. The Washington Institute seeks to promote democratic principles which affirm the inherent value, freedom, and responsibility of the individual, the integrity of the family and the interdependence of the community of man. The Institute researches a broad range of public policy options, recognizing that the individual, the government and private social institutions share the responsibility for the common welfare—including the maintenance of a strong national defense. Policy options are generally viewed in light of their impact on the individual and the family. To encourage more informed decision-making on public policy issues, the Institute offers its research and resources to scholars, policymakers and the public.

ADDITIONAL TITLES

Beyond Constructive Engagement: United States Policy Toward Africa
Edited by Elliott P. Skinner (1986)

Human Rights in East Asia: A Cultural Perspective
Edited by James C. Hsiung (1986)

The Nuclear Connection: A Reassessment of Nuclear Power and Nuclear Proliferation
Edited by Alvin Weinberg, Marcelo Alonso and Jack N. Barkenbus (1985)

Central America in Crisis
Edited by Marcelo Alonso (1984)

Global Policy: Challenge of the 80's
Edited by Morton A. Kaplan (1984)

THE ECONOMICS OF MASS MIGRATION IN THE TWENTIETH CENTURY

Edited by Sidney Klein

89-097

A WASHINGTON INSTITUTE BOOK

PARAGON HOUSE PUBLISHERS

NEW YORK

Published in the United States by
PARAGON HOUSE PUBLISHERS
2 Hammarskjöld Plaza
New York, New York 10017

Designed by *Paul Chevannes*

A Washington Institute for Values in Public Policy Book

Library of Congress Cataloging-in-Publication Data

The Economics of Mass Migration in The Twentieth Century.

Bibliography
Includes index.
1. Emigration and immigration—Economic aspects—History—20th century.
I. Klein, Sidney, 1923-

JV6118.E28   1986   331.12'7'0904   86-16945
ISBN 0-88702-212-X
      0-88702-213-8 (pbk.)

CONTENTS

THE ECONOMICS OF MASS MIGRATION: AN INTRODUCTION

Sidney Klein

Mass migrations go back millions of years. Over many millenia the names, places, causes, consequences and the *modus operandi* of immigrations have changed but the essential characteristics of the phenomenon have remained the same. Whether it has been the "pull" of economic opportunities and/or political and religious freedom in a new land or the "push" of extremely harsh economic, political, social, military and/or religious circumstances in a homeland, the fact is that many peoples and people have moved in numbers that were significant at the time. They packed as much human, physical, and financial capital as possible into the transport available and left to create a new life in another place. Perhaps a temporary economic vacuum was created in the lands left behind and an economic vacuum, however small in some cases, was filled in the lands occupied. Of course, other non–economic changes also occurred; and history of all non–economic types was made as well.

To place the economic consequences of mass migration in the late twentieth century in historical perspective, it is useful to review briefly a list of some earlier migrations. Given the qualitative and quantitative inadequacy of the historical data available, the list undoubtedly errs on the side of omission. In addition, there are problems of definitions and/or categories. For example, do people who ultimately became emigrants have to have begun with the intent of migration to be considered as immigrants? How does one categorize soldiers who, at the conclusion of military operations in foreign areas, did not return to their homeland, either voluntarily or involuntarily? In the same vein, how does one categorize traders who, at the conclusion of a commercial trading operation in a foreign land, did not return to their homeland? Similarly, how does one categorize slaves who, since time immemorial, have been involuntarily moved from nation to nation? Further, what is the difference between "migration" and "mass migration"? What proportion of a "losing" country's population or a "gaining" country's population does a group of migrants have to be for the movement to be considered a "mass migration"?

In preparing a list of migrations in the recorded early history of mankind, I have not attempted to deal with such matters. The list is not intended to be complete but rather simply an indication that international migrations have been occurring on this planet for at least 4000 years and are likely to continue far into the future; and given improvements in transportation and communications, perhaps at an accelerated rate. The list of long past migrations indicates why contemporary migrations warrant close study. Let us look at the record.

In Mesopotamia, as long ago as the period 2000 B.C. to 1500 B.C., there were migrations involving Assyrians, Hittites, and Hurrians. In that same period, the Hyksos migrated to Egypt from what is now Syria or Israel. In Asia there was movement from central Asia toward and into what is now China. Concurrently, Indo-Europeans were migrating in large numbers into India. In the next 500 years, in the Middle East, migrations were recorded involving Assyria, Mitanni, Egypt (e.g., the well known exodus of Jews), Israel, Babylonia, and the Phyrgians, Hittites, Arameans, and Philistines. The motives for these migrations were mixed but most frequently were related to military matters.

From 1000 B.C. to 500 B.C., voluntary and involuntary migrations in the Mediterranean area and in the Middle East that were recorded involved: Dorians, Ionians, Phoenicians, Arians, Acharians, Assyrians, Medians, Jews, Etruscans, Romans, Trojans,

Spartans, Chalcians, Corinthians, Cimmerians, Mannians, Boetians, Miletusians, Megarans, Therans, Alarodoins, Tibarenians, Moschians, Cappadocians, Armenians, Persians, and Phocians. Equally unfamiliar names appear on a list of migrant peoples for the period 500 B.C. to the beginning of the Christian era: Miletusians, Gauls, Poseidonians, Lucanians, Antibesians, Niceans, Denians, Celts, Medians, Sarmatians, Romans, Huns, Yuechians, Sakas, Tocharians, Cimbians, Teutones, Suebians, and Boiians.

In the first 500 years of the Christian calendar, the migrations recorded involved Marcomannis, Huns, Goths, Alanis, Dacians, Egyptians, Quadians, Ruigis, Burgundians, Tungus, Romans, Visigoths, Suebis, Vandals, Salian Franks, Arians, Angles, Saxons, Jutes, Aquileans, Ostrogoths, and Hephalites.

From 500 A.D. to 1000 A.D. migrations recorded involved Lombards, Angles, Saxons, Picts, Celtic Britons, Slavs, Bulgars, Kotriguris, Utriguris, (Central and South) Americans, Avars, Khazars, Greeks, Arabs, Nardites, Syrians, Armenians, Mesopotamians, Raiateans, Tibetans, Vikings, Uighurs, Khirghisans, Slavs, Finno-Ugrians, Norwegians, and Magyars.

In the next 500 years, from 1000 A.D. to 1500 A.D., the following groups are involved in migrations: Toltecs, Normans, Chichimechs, Mongols, Thais, Germans, Jews and Turks. From 1500 A.D. to the present, the groups which have migrated bear names more familiar to most people: Spaniards, Portuguese, Italians, Germans, Russians, Turks, Jews, English, Dutch, French, Manchus, Chinese, Japanese, Koreans, Indians, Viet Namese, Cambodians, Laotians, Mexicans, Columbians, Salvadorans, Panamanians, Haitians, Cubans, Puerto Ricans, Samoans, Pakistanis, Bengalis, Iranians, Lebanese, Egyptians, Palestinians, Yemenis, Afghans, and blacks from a long list of African tribes, regions, and nations. As the list suggests, since 1500 A.D., but especially in the last half of the twentieth century, many nations on this planet have experienced inflows or outflows of people and encountered the costs and benefits of those processes.

In recognition of the current and growing importance of world mass migration in the late twentieth century and in particular those which may affect the United States, the Washington Institute for Values in Public Policy sponsored a conference on "The Economic Consequences of World Mass Migration" which was held in Washington, D.C., January 12-13, 1985. Dr. C. Lowell Harriss was honorary chairman of the conference while I served as coordinating chairman. Economists representing a wide variety of institutions and points of view delivered papers on the diverse geographic and functional aspects of the subject. Constructive spirited discussions ensued. The papers and conference were intended to be fresh looks at age–old processes in new historic settings. Five of the papers are published in this volume. It needs to be emphasized that each of the papers represents the views of the author and does not necessarily reflect the views of the officers, staff, and trustees of The Washington Institute or those of Professor Harriss or mine. Those of us involved in the administration of the conference and publication of the papers had no preconceived ideas or positions to advocate; nor have we now. Our role is solely to further objective research; and hence indirectly to contribute information to be used by others as they see fit in the formulation of national immigration policy in various countries, including and especially the USA.

The first paper in this volume, "Benefits and Costs of Migration" by Dr. Edwin P. Reubens provides an analytical framework for discussion of the economic issues involved. He constructs taxonomies of economic benefits and offsets for both the countries of immigration and emigration with special reference to the USA. In addition, there are insightful references to the experiences and problems of other countries and areas. His paper deals with such functional matters as magnitudes of immigration; modes of entry and types of immigrants; skilled workers; unskilled workers; and capacity to absorb foreign workers. With only minor modifications to fit individual national economies, his taxonomies have world wide applications.

In the next four papers, a relatively narrower geographic approach is adopted and the emphasis changes to countries other than the USA. In the paper on "Koreans in America: Recent Migration From South Korea to the United States," Dr. Paul W. Kuznets focuses on just one group of immigrants, i.e. South Koreans, whose number in the USA has increased dramatically in recent years and is likely to continue to do so. Dr. Kuznets analyzes the reasons for their migration and the economic effects in South Korea, a small country with a population of only 41 million in 1984. In the third paper, Dr. M.C. Madhaven writes about "Indian Emigration: Its Demension and Impact on Indian Economy." He deals with the economic effects of migration on a country with a land area one–third that of the United States (1.3 million square miles vs. 3.6 million square miles for the USA) but a population over three times that of the USA (763 million vs. 240 million for the USA in 1985). Interestingly, while there were perhaps 500,000 plus South Koreans in the USA in 1985, there were probably only about 200,000 plus immigrants from India living here at that time. As with South Koreans and other groups of migrants, the number of Indian immigrants to the USA and other nations too may be expected to increase in the next decade or so. Dr. Madhaven examines the dimensions of Indian emigration worldwide, the causes of emigration, and the impact on the economy of India; and as with Dr. Kuznets, employs some of the analytical techniques discussed in Dr. Reubens' paper.

The fourth paper, "Economic Impact of European Migration to Latin America After World War II," by Dr. Norman Plotkin analyzes Spanish, Italian, Portuguese and other European migrations to Argentina, Brazil, Venezuela and other Latin American Nations. He contrasts the economic milieu in Latin America with that of the USA and further contrasts the pre-World War II and post–World War II migrations from Europe to Latin America. He too employs by now familiar criteria to evaluate the economic consequences of the migrations.

The fifth paper by Dr. John F. Walker deals with the migration experiences of Australia and New Zealand. Under-populated and underdeveloped, and with an ethnic mix and a history of racially oriented immigration policies similar in many ways to that of the USA, the Australian and New Zealand experiences seem to parallel those of the USA in a number of respects. However, there are major differences vis-a-vis the USA with respect to the physically remote location of the two "down under" nations; their consequent greater control over immigration, and their recent interest in stimulating immigration for defense as well as for economic purposes. The techniques of migration control practiced in Australia and New Zealand are certainly very different from the USA.

As suggested previously, these five papers deal with the tip of an iceberg which is rapidly becoming more visible to the world. Much work remains to be done on mass migrations on global, regional, and national bases. As transportation and communications continue to improve dramatically world wide and as large numbers of people react to all sorts of "pulls" and "pushes," it will become increasingly important for nations to know in advance what the economic costs and benefits of those migrations will be. It is much more cost effective to first measure, and then predict and control mass movements internationally in advance of their occurrence than to try to deal with them after the fact. Let us hope that nations can learn from the past. I believe these papers are a step in that direction.

CHAPTER 1
BENEFITS AND COSTS OF MIGRATION

Edwin P. Reubens

Introduction

In the prolific literature on international migration, it is common to find more opinions than evidence on the effects of immigration and emigration, including particularly strong judgments with weak support as to benefits and burdens to the countries of departure and of entry. These judgments are seldom aware of the criteria and principles they use. They rarely address all the relevant experience pro and con some *a priori* position, let alone weighing the qualitatively diverse gross effects of migration so as to arrive at net outcomes.[1]

The process and effects of migration are very complex and range widely across the economies and societies concerned. However, that is no excuse for the many tendentious and unscientific treatments of migration by various special interests. More rational, rigorous, and public–spirited treatment is sorely needed.

On the face of it, international migration lends itself to arguments that are almost equally plausible as to net benefits or net burdens. The U.S., for example, is often said to gain from immigration: obtaining an increment of workers to fill vacancies in certain "low-level" jobs, also gaining a restraint on general wage inflation, and a slowdown of the exodus of labor–intensive industries. However, the U.S. is also said to be harmed by immigration: suffering an increase in unemployment, downward pressures on wage levels, delays in advancing technology and productivity, and the burden of foreign workers' remittances on the balance of international payments. By the same token, Taiwan for example might be said to gain from emigration: relief of population pressure, receipt of remittances from abroad, eventual return of some emigrants bringing accumulated savings and work experience. But, Taiwan might also be said to suffer from emigration: loss of professional and skilled workers, disruption of local economy and society by departing and returning migrants.

Wherever there is such a pattern of plausible but qualitatively diverse benefits and costs, there is clear need to develop an explicit model, which will direct attention to all the relevant empirical facts, and which will also designate a consistent method of measuring and inter-relating them.

Toward a Cost/Benefit Model of Migration

The question of the economic consequences of international migration—as with any other phenomenon that strikes an on–going economic system—can be approached on many levels. The micro–level is concerned with demand and supply relations in production, pricing, and factor payment in the short run. The macro–level concerns disequilibria and readjustments in the aggregate and over the course of the business cycle. The secular trends comprise stimulus–response mechanisms, evolving structures, and long-term processes. Distributional considerations deal with the gains and losses of individuals, groups, classes, and localities, within the aggregate, and extending into social and moral criteria of distributional outcomes. The economic significance of migration must be pursued in all these wide ranges and some remote corners of any economic system which the migrants leave and enter.

In order not to get lost in this vast terrain, we will take an operational approach to "migration," focusing on the effects of migration without losing sight of the relevant causes of migration. First we will treat Immigration into the receiving countries, which nowadays are mostly advanced industrial nations (more developed countries, or MDCs), and preeminently the United States of America. Then we will treat Emigration from the source countries, which nowadays are mostly less developed countries (or LDCs). Then the international interactions and outcomes will be consolidated, to suggest a net world sum of benefits/ costs.

By the same token, we propose an operational definition of the "economic consequences" of migration, in terms of increments/ decrements in population, labor force, unemployment, earnings, vacancies, output, technologic change, industrial innovation, usage of social facilities, and consumption of goods and services. These increments and decrements, in the various magnitudes, qualities, and rates of change, can then be evaluated as to the costs and benefits they are found to bring to the countries at issue. Thus we reformulate the initial question as: Does Immigration/Emigration bring a net social burden or a net social dividend?

We can try to answer that question by relating the increments/ decrements empirically to each country's "needs" for inflows/ outflows of people, and to its "capacity to absorb" such inflows/outflows (N/CA model).[2] Here "need" means "an excess of labor demand over supply at current prices," and is usually indicated by a tendency for wages to rise while vacancies persist. Likewise, "capacity to absorb" is defined as "an excess of supply of social facilities over demand at current prices," and is usually indicated by little or no rise of "prices" as the demand increases. The "prices" here may include budgetary costs, tax rates, crowding and queues, cultural conflicts, and the like.

The model must also take some account of the causes of migrations, since those causes may help to explain the nature, intensity, and duration of the effects that are our prime subject. We therefore adopt an Aspirations/Opportunities/Mobility (A/O/M) model, according to which migration occurs when there is sufficient increase in the aspirations of people, and/or in the relative opportunities they perceive abroad and at home, and in the conditions of feasible mobility. This is to say that location, for most people and at most times, remains as is under prevailing conditions of aspirations, opportunities, and mobility. However, location will be changed as a result of some positive change in those three conditions, whether in all of them or in some permutation yielding a positive net effect. Analytically:

$$L = f(A, O, M) \text{, and}$$
$$dL = f'(dA, dO, dM).$$

We are here formulating a "disequilibrium system," consisting of imbalances of supply and demand, that persist beyond short –run adjustments, and generate longer-term processes. The most important features of the disequilibrium of Migration are: in the MDCs, the persistence of low–level job vacancies; and in the LDCs, the persistence of surplus labor, on the skilled and the unskilled levels.

Taxonomy of Immigration Impacts and their Benefits or Offsets

The foregoing analytic schema is embodied in the following tabulation of the effects of immigration in a receiving country (mostly MDCs). Listed on the lefthand side are the several increments brought by an inflow of people; and on the righthand side are the corresponding potential effects, treated as specific benefits of immigration or as burdens offset in some degree, over subsequent years. This tabulation represents the initial impact of a given inflow and the subsequent economic and social adjust-ments, all abstracted from the ongoing arrivals of new inflows every year.

The immigrants are broadly distinguished as to "PTK", namely "professional, technical and kindred" workers, according to the usage of the U.S. Immigration and Naturalization Service (INS); and the "UML," who are "unskilled mass laborers." Some finer breakdowns appear below.

A corresponding treatment of the effects of emigration upon the source countries (mostly LDCs) is presented in the section regard-ing effects of emigration.

The Effects of Immigration

This part of the paper deals with the actual effects of immigration into MDCs, in terms of available evidence and functional rela-tions, under six sub-heads: Magnitudes of Immigration; Modes of Entry and Types of Immigrants; Skilled Workers: numbers and need for PTK; Unskilled Workers; numbers of UML; Need for Unskilled Workers; and Capacity to Absorb Foreign Workers.

Magnitudes of Immigration

Basic to all discussions of the significance of immigration into any area is the much-vexed question of the numbers; or more exactly the absolute and relative magnitudes of the stocks and flows of alien workers, broken down by levels of skill and channels of movement. Enumerations are needed for three main categories: the legal immigrants (in which are included the authorized refugees), the temporary workers (authorized admissions for limited periods), and the illegal aliens (the "undocumented workers" who enter the country surreptitiously, or overstay their authorized limited-period entry). In all these categories, our main emphasis will fall on skills brought and occupations pursued by the entrants.

For the United States of America, which receives the largest inflows in the world, the data are firm only for the gross inflows of the first two categories of entrants. (In the annual statistics on "legal immigrants", 70-80 percent are "new arrivals" holding visas for permanent residence, the others representing "adjustments of status" for previous temporary entrants who are granted permanent residence permits in the given year.) Little is known about the return flow of legal entrants or the outflow of native citizens; and much less is known about the gross entries and the return flow of illegals. The available data must therefore be supplemented by estimates applying plausible ratios on apprehensions, duplications and evasions, return–flows and direct emigration, labor–force participation, representativeness of small samples, and other features. Accordingly, the existing estimates vary widely; showing a swing from older tendencies of magnifying the numbers and alleged dangers of immigration, down to recent tendencies of some commentators to minimize both the accumulated stock and the current net inflows of migrants. As an extreme example, the population of illegal aliens in the U.S. in the late 1970s was estimated at anywhere from 2 million persons to 8 or even 12 million.

My own estimates—using reasonable middle–of–the–road ratios, and focused on actual workers—find that the "recently accumulated" total stock of all aliens (legal and illegal, accumulated over the preceding five years) who were in the labor force of the U.S. in 1978 was about 4 million workers; and in 1983 (10-year accumulation) was probably close to 8 million workers. Correspondingly, my estimate puts the annual net inflow of workers, legal and illegal, in the order of 900,000 a year in recent years.[3]

A TAXONOMY OF IMMIGRATION EFFECTS

Foreign Increments	Benefits or Offsets
1) Additional population	Mostly workers, relatively few dependents.[a]
2) Additional workers	Either PTK for high-level vacancies, or unskilled workers for low-level job but stay-ons soon move up.
3) Additional job-seekers	Little unemployment of Aliens, and no Unemployment Compensation for most of them; but unemployment may rise for natives if displaced by aliens.
4) Acceptance of reduced wages and working conditions	Depends on displacement effects, segregated shops, unionization, enforcement of minimum wage law and safety laws, unemployment compensation, other support.
5) Delay of technological progress and industrial innovation	Depends partly on effects in (4);[b] also preserves jobs, postpones industrial demise.
6) Additional use of social facilities:	
Housing	Rent payments, use of low-level housing;
Transportation	Fare payments;
Public Schools, Public Health, Police, Fire, Courts, Public Welfare	Payment of taxes (sales, property, income payroll tax, FICA payments); low utilization of these facilities;
Social Security benefits	FICA paid but few benefits collected.
7) Additional consumption in retail markets	Payments out of earnings; but high rate of saving by most of the immigrants (anti-inflationary), but high remittances abroad (dollar outflow).
8) Additional minority groups and cultures	Cultural diversity and enrichment. but also conflicts.

[a] The legally admitted aliens can bring more dependents later, under family-preference visas or off-quota altogether.

[b] However, many technological improvements are introduced because they economize even on low wages.

TABLE 1
GROSS ADMISSIONS OF IMMIGRANTS INTO NORTH
AMERICA, 1951–1984

U.S.A.		Canada	
1951-1960	2,515,479	1951	194,391
1951	205,717	1952	164,498
1952	265,520	1953	168,868
1953	170,434	1954	154,227
1954	208,177	1955	109,946
1955	237,790	1956	164,857
1956	321,625	1957	282,164
1957	326,867	1958	124,851
1958	253,265	1959	106,928
1959	260,686	1960	104,111
1960	265,398	1961	71,689
		1962	74,586
1961-1970	3,321,677	1963	93,151
1961	271,344	1964	112,606
1962	283,763	1965	146,758
1963	306,260	1966	194,743
1964	292,248	1967	222,876
1965	296,697	1968	183,974
1966	323,040	1969	161,531
1967	361,972	1970	147,713
1968	454,448	1971	121,900
1969	358,579	1972	122,006
1970	373,326	1973	184,200
		1974	218,465
1971-1980	4,493,314	1975	187,881
1971	370,478	1976	149,429
1972	384,685	1977	114,914
1973	400,063	1978	86,313
1974	394,861	1979	112,096
1975	386,194	1980	143,117
1976	398,613	1981	128,618
1976, TQ	103,676	1982	121,147
1977	462,315	1983	89,157
1978	601,442	1984	n.a.
1979	460,348		
1980	530,639		
1981	596,600		
1982	594,131		
1983	567,645		
1984	543,903		

SOURCES: for U.S.A.—*Statistical Yearbook of the Immigration and Naturalization Service, 1981;* and F.A.I.R, *Information Exchange,* April 11, 1985.
for Canada—*Immigration Statistics,* Ministry of Employment and Immigration, 1983.

Relating these aggregate numbers to the corresponding American magnitudes, we find that the recently accumulated stock of alien workers amounts to only about 7.1 percent of the whole labor force in the United States. The dramatic comparison, however, is that with the number of unemployed; approximately 8 million persons in 1984, it is almost exactly equalled by the alien stock of workers here. Furthermore, if the U.S. unemployment figure is written down by about 3 to 4 million for unavoidable, partly optional "labor float" in this mobile society (roughly equivalent to the so–called "natural rate of unemployment,") the estimated real shortfall of jobs becomes 4 to 5 million;[4] and the alien stock comes to approximately double the real shortfall. But counting discouraged dropouts would enlarge the total shortfall. In addition, the aggregate unemployment indicated here is concentrated among particular groups in U.S. society, notably teenagers, the aged, housewives newly entering or reentering the labor force, and ethnic and social minorities; and is likewise concentrated in the older cities of the Northeast region and Northcentral older industries.

In a similar comparison using the flow data, the net inflow of aliens, in my estimate of .9 million a year, adds not quite 1 percent to the U.S. labor force annually. Yet in a more dynamic comparison with the annual growth of 2 million in the reported labor force, the net alien inflow amounts to virtually half of that measured increment.

Corresponding measures for Canada refer only to legal immigration, as little is known about illegal entries except that they probably are in a far smaller ratio to the legal admissions each year than is found in the U.S. Gross admissions into Canada have varied widely over the past two decades (largely as a function of changing official regulations and quotas). Since 1970, the gross admissions have mostly ranged between 112,000 and 150,000 annually, with a few lower and a few higher figures, averaged to about 137,000 a year.[5] Emigration from Canada, however, is high; estimated at about 63,500 persons in 1978, such that the net inflow was not quite 70,000 a year on an average, and only about 80,000 each year in 1981 and 1982. This amounts to a net increment of barely .3 of 1 percent in Canada's present population. The net inflow looks large only if it is related to the annual growth of Canada's population, where it accounts for about 25-30 percent each year.[6]

In the case of Western Europe, admissions for permanent settlement are few, and are generally restricted to outstanding personages, unusual skills, or special refugees. The chief inflow has been "guest workers," admitted in large numbers from the 1950s until about 1973, under contracts for authorized temporary stays. At their high tide, about 800,000 a year—mostly from LDCs around the Mediterranean basin—were admitted to relieve domestic shortages of labor. After 1973, however, economic slowdown led the European governments to close this door; and to encourage, even subsidize, return flows, which nevertheless have been reluctant and meager.

The accumulated stocks of foreign labor, as of 1977/78, are shown in the accompanying Table 2, with relative proportions taken against actual civilian employment figures. This table indicates, for that date and with little change to the present, that for these countries—excluding Canada (population figures, not workers), and except for unusual Switzerland—foreign workers account for 4 to 8 percent of their total civilian employment. Their unemployment rates—which were formerly very low in all these countries, except the U.S. with moderately low rates—have climbed until in 1984 they range from nearly zero (Switzerland), through 8 to 9 per cent (Germany, France), to 15 percent (Belgium and Netherlands).[7]

Modes of Entry and Types of Immigrants

As mentioned above, there are three or four main categories of immigrants according to mode of entry into the U.S., Canada, and western Europe. We consider first the legal immigrants, who enter under a system of quotas and preferences administered by the issuance of visas and inspection at the borders.

The present U.S. system, as amended to date, admits some on–quota, off–quota, refugees, and temporary workers. The quota comprises a single, worldwide ceiling of 290,000 visas distributed annually in accordance with seven limited preferences (see Table 3 for a list of these preferences and their respective limits). Of these preferences, the third and sixth—each comprising not more than 10 percent of the total visas—relate to occupations and labor supply/demand: each visa application under these preferences is subject to certification by the U.S. Department of Labor showing that a labor shortage exists for the specified occupation. The other preferences apply to various family relationships; to U.S. citizens or to lawful alien residents; or refer to authorized refugees from foreign countries. The total visas under the worldwide annual

TABLE 2
STOCKS OF FOREIGN WORKERS
AND
TOTAL WORKERS
EIGHT DEVELOPED COUNTRIES,
1977/1978, AND CANADA 1981

Country	(1) Foreign Workers[a] (000s)	(2) Total Civilian Employment[c] (000s)	(3) Percentage (1) ÷ (2)
Austria	176.7	2,700	6.5
Belgium	306.3	4,500	6.8
France	1,642.8	20,962	7.8
Germany (F.R.)	1,961.9	24,511	8.0
Netherlands	196.4	4,555	4.3
Sweden	224.5	4,099	5.5
Switzerland	489.4	2,817	17.4
United States[b] (authorized (unauthorized	4,200.0 1,200.0 3,000.0)	90,546	4.6
Canada	3,867[d]	24,083[e]	16.1

[a] The foreign workers in the seven European countries listed here mostly originated in less developed countries (LDCs) and were mostly admitted for authorized temporary stays. Unauthorized foreign workers may add another 10 percent.
SOURCE: *OECD Observer*, May 1980.

[b] The figures for foreign workers in the U.S. represent a net accumulation over the preceding five years, as described in footnote 3.

[c] Total civilian employment figures in mid-1977 for five European countries and the United States, as reported in *OECD Observer*, March 1979. Figures for Austria and Belgium estimated in terms of reported population and comparable employment rates.

[d] Foreign-born population, 1981.

[e] Total population, 1981.

ceiling of 290,000 is further limited to no more than 20,000 per country of origin—regardless of country size or its particular circumstances, except for additional specially authorized refugees. Actual admissions under that ceiling usually run somewhat less than 290,000 annually.

TABLE 3
PREFERENCE SYSTEM U.S. IMMIGRATION ACT OF 1965 GOVERNING ADMISSIONS UNDER CEILINGS[a]

1. First preference: Unmarried sons and daughters of U.S. citizens.
   Not more than 20 percent of admissions under ceilings.

2. Second preference: Spouse and unmarried sons and daughters of an alien lawfully admitted for permanent residence.
   20 percent plus any not required for first preference.

3. Third preference: Members of the professions and scientists and artists of exceptional ability.
   Not more than 10 percent.

4. Fourth preference: Married sons and daughters of U.S. citizens.
   10 percent plus any not required for first three preferences.

5. Fifth preference: Brothers and sisters of U.S. citizens.[b]
   24 percent plus any not required for first four preferences.

6. Sixth preference: Skilled and unskilled workers in occupations for which labor is in short supply in the United States.
   Not more than 10 percent.

7. Seventh preference: Refugees to whom conditional entry or adjustment of status may be granted.
   Not more than 6 percent.[c]

8. Nonpreference: Any applicant not entitled to one of the above preferences.
   Any numbers not required for preference applicants.

[a] Revised from C. Keely, U.S. Immigration: A Policy Analysis (The Population Council, 1979), p. 21.

[b] The citizens must be over 21 years of age, according to amendment in 1976.

[c] Additional refugees may be admitted under special acts of Congress and under the "parole power" of the Attorney General.

Another kind of inflow consists of the parents, spouses and children of adult U.S. citizens, who are admitted under exemption from any ceilings. These run close to 300,000 a year, of which newly arrived aliens are less than half (the others being "adjustments of aliens already in this country").

Still another inflow consists of "temporary" workers in approved occupations, admitted for periods of a few months up to several years, either as "exchange visitors" (mostly high-level professionals: about 30,000 a year in recent years), or as "H–1s" (also high-level: 16,000 a year), or as "H–2" workers (mostly farm labor but also other skills: about 21,000 a year, no dependents). Inflows of such temporary workers in any year are largely offset by the outflows in that year, so they are mostly a "revolving stock" making only a small accumulation.

As regards controlling foreign additions to the U.S. labor force, the foregoing system in principle limits specified foreign workers with stated occupations to no more than 58,000 immigrant visas annually, or little more than 10 percent of the approximately 530,000 total authorized admissions each year nowadays. However, in reality the only labor limit is the labor–force participation of all those annually entering as immigrants, whether they are on–quota immigrants or are off–quota relatives and refugees.

The illegal entrants are, of course, uncontrolled as to numbers and occupations. Sample studies[8] indicate that they have a very high labor–participation rate, and are mostly unskilled persons. They seek and find lowlevel jobs which they can quickly learn to do by actually doing them. There are only a few, rather over–publicized, cases of illegals taking wellpaid or highlevel positions.

The system of immigration control used in Canada is not very different in principle from the one used in the U.S. It provides for a smaller total admission, of course, and gives more emphasis to labor–market criteria. Under legislation which came into effect in 1978, points are assigned to an applicant on the basis of family sponsorship, language abilities, occupational needs of the economy, and region of intended settlement. In 1980, of 143,000 total admissions of "landed immigrants," nearly 64,000 were workers in declared occupations; and of these, the three largest classes —with just over 14,000 in each class—were: professional and technical; clerical, sales, and services; and operatives.[9]

The west European system is, as already mentioned, quite different from that of North America. Immigration for settlement in western Europe is very restricted and very small. Since 1955, almost all the inflows have been contractual guest–workers. It was originally planned to keep out their dependents, and to stop and reverse the flow as needed. However, family unification was soon permitted, and this deepened the reluctance to repatriate. When new admissions were suspended in the 1970s, illegal entries increased, amounting today to perhaps a 10 percent addition to the alien stock resident there.

Skilled Foreign Workers: Numbers and the Need for them

In the high–skill category, mostly designated in the U.S. as PTK (professional, technical, and kindred), the predominant sub-classes are doctors, nurses, engineers, scientists, managers, per-formers in the arts and sports, teachers, craftsmen, etc. Their flow nowadays is mostly from certain LDCs to certain MDCs, either as immigrants for settlement there or as limited–stay workers (some as temporary workers for periods of up to one year, others as visiting professionals for periods usually up to two or three years).

The U.S. has been, by far, the chief destination: in the early 1970s, for example, when the U.S. accepted for immigration about 39,000 PTKs from LDCs annually, and 49,000 PTKs from all foreign countries, the numbers were three times the correspond-ing number accepted by Canada, and over forty times for the U.K. acceptances. By 1979, the number was down to 39,000 accepted by the U.S. from all countries, but fell still more in the other MDCs. Besides the immigrant PTK, the U.S. admits even larger numbers for short stays (H–1 visas for one year, and exchange visitor visas for 1 to 3 years). The chief source countries for PTK have been in Asia; predominantly the Philippines, India, Korea, and Taiwan.

PTK are trained and experienced persons, mostly in their middle years, although a few are young adults and some are senior people. Those who come seeking professional posts and large incomes in the host countries are usually fleeing from the over-supply and meager incomes of those professions in their home countries. When migrating for settlement, they usually bring their dependents; some do so even for rather short stays. Accordingly they send home relatively small amounts of remittances, in view of their large incomes and in comparison with the behavior of other immigrant groups discussed below. On the other hand, many PTK accumulate large savings during their stay in the host country for transfer home in accordance with their plans for return. Estimates of return flow rates suggest that in the 1970s about one–fourth of the gross annual inflow of PTK immigrants into the U.S. was offset by PTK return flows.[10]

Professional inflows might have a strong impact upon the receiving nation if professionals entered in such large numbers as to depress fees and earnings, thereby benefiting the consumers of their services but hurting the native professionals. As it happens however, the size and fields of the PTK inflow are mostly controlled by the mechanisms of admission. In the U.S., those who enter for permanent settlement under occupational preferences (mostly under the Third Preference in the immigration law) must obtain certification from the Labor Department that a specific vacancy exists; those who enter for limited stay (mostly on H–1 visas as Temporary Workers or on J–1 visas as exchange visitors) are authorized only in the light of existing needs for short–period stays. Canada's controls are roughly similar.

To be sure, the immigration authorities may underestimate or overestimate the need for foreign professionals in any particular field. Some professionals can enter a country under its general immigration quotas, or under refugee quotas, or in off–quota categories, all without occupational preference, and then pursue that profession to the point of conflict with native personnel. In the U.S. in recent years, the inflow of foreign PTK has been protested by the acting profession, the medical profession, some sports circles, as well as a few others.

On the other hand, foreign PTK have often been found to fill vacancies of a very stubborn and difficult kind, notably medical posts in inner–city hospitals and clinics and in nursing homes and old age homes, all of which have great trouble recruiting native interns and physicians for their house staff. Thus in recent years, foreign medical graduates (FMGs) constitute about 30 percent of the resident medical staff in all hospitals in the United States and over half in New York City's municipal hospitals. The immigrant gross inflow of PTK recently has been adding about one–fourth of 1 percent annually to this country's stock of professional personnel. This amounts to about 3 percent of the annual rate of increase of that whole stock. However, for physicians in particular, until the large expansion of U.S. medical schools in the 1970s and the sharp curtailment of FMG entries decreed by Congress in 1976, the annual entries of FMGs in the early 1970s were making up fully half of the entire increase in the supply of physicians, and FMGs were still filling vacancies at the end of the decade.[11] (The FMGs include immigrants plus exchange visitors on 1 to 3 year stays plus Americans with foreign medical degrees.)

The gain to advanced countries that are short of labor—overall or for particular occupations—and receive foreign inflows, consists not only in the support of operations and the restraint of costs, but also in obtaining these gains at virtually zero investment cost. That is, they obtain a valuable asset—"human capital" developed elsewhere at considerable expense—which is transferred at no direct charge or compensation. Thus the MDCs gain from immigration the whole of the "avoided costs of nurture and education" that they would have incurred if they had raised and trained the equivalent number of native workers and professionals. Even if the costs of sheer nurture are set aside as reflecting family choices that would operate in the MDC in any case, at the least the avoided cost of education (ACE) for the imported PTK may be estimated. Thus, in the peak period centered on 1971, for annual PTK inflow into the U.S. from LDCs, the corresponding ACE is estimated at about $500 million (in then current dollars), or about 2 percent of the total expenditure on higher education in the U.S. in that year. It may also be assessed as 15 percent of U.S. official development assistance to LDCs in that year.[12]

Although the contributions of foreign PTK to the host society are often recognized, and sometimes exaggerated, criticisms of this migration mostly focus on the effects upon the countries of origin: the emigration is said to be a "brain drain" that severely damages welfare and development in the LDCs. Whether such damage occurs depends on the actual conditions as to shortage or surplus of PTK in the various LDCs of emigration, and return flow of remittances, etc.—a subject which is treated below, in the Emigration section of this paper.

Unskilled Foreign Workers

Whereas professionals almost always enter through legitimate channels, and at worst some of them overstay their authorization period, the unskilled entrants must be considered in a four-fold classification: legal and illegal entrants, both permanent and temporary.

In the U.S. case, where skilled and semi-skilled persons accounted for about 25 percent of total authorized permanent immigration in the mid-1970s, and about 30 percent at the end of the 1970s, the remainder was made up of UML: laborers, service workers and other workers. Together with the large group of housewives, children and unclassified persons, this group accounted for over half of the authorized total. In Canada in 1980 the proportion of skilled and semi–skilled persons in the total authorized immigration was likewise about 30 percent, leaving the remainder for the unskilled and out–of–the–labor–force group, similar to the U.S. but somewhat differently composed.

As regards authorized but temporary entries of unskilled persons, these come into the U.S. mainly through the H–2 program. The annual numbers were only about 30,000 in the mid-1970s, and were reduced to only 21,000 by the end of the 1970s. There is almost no accumulation of these because nearly all are returned to their home countries within one year. One large group of these aliens is employed mostly in fruit picking, sugar cane cutting, and sheepherding—all occupations that native Americans tend to shun. Other H–2s are employed in relatively small numbers in a wide variety of skilled and semi–skilled special occupations and work locations. The Department of Labor supervises their employment to safeguard prevailing wages and working conditions.

In Western Europe, the much larger inflows of "guest workers" have gone predominantly into manufacturing, in a rising trend. In West Germany by 1970 about 63 percent of the guest workers were in this field, where they accounted for 13 percent of the whole workforce there. Another important field for guest workers in that country in 1970 was construction, where only 17 percent of them were employed but accounted for 17 percent of that whole field. Other industries engaged much smaller percentages. The aggregate (average) share of foreigners was 8.7 percent of the whole workforce in West Germany. These magnitudes and allocations reflect, as an I.L.O. scholar puts it, "the ubiquitous existence of socially undesirable jobs and the adaptation of labour demand under shortage conditions."[13]

The largest and most distressing of the alien inflows are the illegal movements, which are most prominent in the case of the U.S. but also occur in other new world countries; also in western Europe (where they add about 10 percent to the resident legal workers). Their length of stay seems to range from a few months' stay to several years to permanent residence, suggesting some accumulation of these persons, together with some home visits at intervals.

There is little direct data on the illegal entrants. Estimates of their annual flows and accumulated stocks in the U.S. are in considerable dispute at the present time. For the U.S., the chief case, estimates of the accumulated stock range from under 2 million to a high of 8 million. A reasonable, middleground estimate is 3 million illegal workers as of 1978 (see note 3), and therefore probably 5-6 million in 1983. Calculating from Immigration and Naturalization Service (INS) annual apprehensions data, adjusted for duplications of apprehended persons, ratios of not –apprehended to apprehended persons, short stays and return flows, and estimated labor–force participation rates, the corresponding net inflow figure for illegal alien workers is 600,000 per year at the present time.[14]

These illegals come mainly from Mexico, across a thinly guarded border 2,000 miles long; and secondarily from the Caribbean islands, with the Spanish–speaking migrants taking particular advantage of the lightly guarded beaches of Puerto Rico as a stepping stone to the U.S. mainland. Additional illegals enter as tourists and others as temporary visitors who then overstay their visas. Some are crewmen who skip ship. Others have bogus authorizations. However, the great majority slip across land or sea borders at night. Covert crossing is usually difficult and hazardous, so it is attempted mostly by young, able–bodied males without dependents, although in recent years more and more young women and some children have been detected, crossing with the aid of the growing number of smuggling rings (known as "coyotes" on the Mexico–U.S. run).

The Need for Foreign Workers of Unskilled Type

Labor market needs for foreigners are most evident in particular branches of low–skilled work, called "low–level jobs," namely the difficult, unpleasant, ill–located, ill–timed, intermittent or part–time, and low–paid jobs, with no promotional prospects, that are staffed disproportionately by aliens, both legal and illegal. Notable examples are found not only in farm work, especially in picking fruits and vegetables, and other outdoor work such as construction; but increasingly in urban and industrial jobs, especially the garment industry, restaurant services, laundries, general cleaning, household service, and a miscellany of manual and service occupations. For many of these low–level jobs, employers claim that native workers simply are not available, or that those who are available under the given conditions and pay are not as productive, reliable, or trainable as aliens. Furthermore, the projections for these kinds of labor in the future show rapid growth in low–level occupations; and according to some experts, "potential surpluses of workers for higher–level occupations and potential shortages for lower–level occupations."[15] Thus there seems to be a marked prospective need for aliens (UML) to fill the vacancies.

The reality of that "need" cannot be entirely accepted at face value. On one hand, it is supported by those who point to underlying reasons for the lack of native workers to fill apparent vacancies; on the other hand, it is attacked by those who look to industrial investment and reorganization to wipe out certain jobs and to upgrade the remaining jobs into attractions for native workers. The former school, arguing on socio–economic lines, and taking the job traits as given, points to the values, attitudes, and "reservation wages" of natives, and the prospects of obtaining superior jobs eventually, together with the available alternatives to working (unemployment compensation, welfare payments, support by family and friends, hustling, crime, and other illicit activities). All these factors imply inelastic supply of native workers for the jobs in question at current wages; and even suggest declining availability or actual withdrawal of native workers (e.g., household workers, migrant farm workers) who are then replaced by foreigners—except perhaps in times of extraordinarily high unemployment.

The opposite school, arguing along the lines of technological and organizational innovation, looks at the particular jobs and their potential transformation.[16] It suggests that some jobs can be eliminated altogether, whether by mechanization and rationalization or by abandoning those particular lines of production. Other jobs can be made attractive by improving their status, wages, and working conditions, especially by raising the official minima as much as may be necessary to attract workers. Any remaining deficiencies in skills can be filled by training additional natives, who will flood the market sufficiently to drive some workers into the less desired posts. The case of Japan, which gets along without alien workers, can be invoked here.[17]

The difference between those two approaches becomes a matter of costs and timing of change within the existing socio–economic structure. Most of the firms where the jobs in question might be indigenized are small in scale, labor–intensive, often intermittent or seasonal in activity, severely competitive, low in profitability, and subject to price–sensitive demand for their product or service. If some of the suggested steps were taken, the result would be rising costs, higher consumer prices, reduced sales and production, increased mechanization of work, and more do–it–yourself household activity (aided by new appliances). There would also be increased migration of firms out of old central-city locations to more remote regions of the country or to foreign locations and the closing of some firms, along with the rise of cheap imports. Most of these tendencies are undesirable in themselves and also reduce jobs for natives as well as aliens.

Over the long run, no doubt, the economy would adjust to the proposed mechanization, upgrading, retraining, and relative price shifts, bringing higher productivity per worker employed, and more equitable distribution of income among those employed. However, a full shift to the Japanese model of respect for low-level work would be slow to accomplish, and unacceptable to many Americans in unions, management, and government. Meanwhile, in the short run there would be reduced and/or relocated employment, aggravated inflation, and intensified trade deficits, with the heaviest burden borne by the most troubled cities and the most disadvantaged groups of citizens. In the end, the jobs at the bottom of the new scale in pay, quality, and prospects might be no more acceptable to native workers than before. If so, they would remain for the aliens, who might be admitted under an accommodative immigration policy—most effectively via a temporary foreign worker policy governed by labor-market criteria.

Capacity to Absorb Foreign Workers

Supposing that foreign workers—both PTK and unskilled—are "needed" in the foregoing senses and in some substantial magnitude, what are the extent and limitations of the "capacity to absorb" them in the economy and society of MDCs?

One of the primal grounds of opposition to foreigners is a matter of population growth, ecology, and pressures on the environment. This is a new concern in the Americas and Australia, which are just now joining the older developed countries of Europe in this concern. While some parties urge MDCs to move toward zero population growth, others point to MDC technology and lifestyle as alternative areas where moves to further absorptive capacity might be made.

At current rates in the U.S., the annual net inflow of over one million aliens—counting both workers and non–workers —amounts to about one–half of one percent of the existing population. This is approximately equal to this country's natural increase. However, if immigration were allowed to rise without limit, drawing from LDC with a combined population of some two and one–half billion, the inflow could become overwhelming. The moral and political dilemma is whether MDC borders should be controlled against the vast outside multitudes and their alleged "natural right to migrate."

Closely related to the demographic problem is the impact of foreign workers on local employment, wages, and working conditions. Assuming as before that the labor-market shows a real "need" for foreign workers, in micro-terms, the consideration of "capacity-to-absorb" focuses on the macro-impact of those aliens who do enter the country: Do they displace natives and do they depress wages?

In a free market, as shown in the accompanying figure, part (a), an inflow of foreign workers shifts the labor supply curve to the right, so that it intersects the given labor demand curve at a lower wage rate and at a larger total volume of employment and output than prevailed before. If the native workers adhere to their original preference schedule, fewer of them will accept jobs at the new lower wage, and the rest of the new work force will be filled in with foreigners. To the native workers, this operation will look like simple job displacement and wage depression by the foreigners at the natives' expense. The natives as workers are, of course, assumed to ignore the benefits that accrue to them as consumers from the reduction in costs that is passed along to them in the form of lower prices as the result of competition and the necessity of disposing of the newly enlarged output.

At the next step, shown in part (b), it is recognized that in a truly free international labor market (as in some naive "open door" proposals now circulating), there would be no end to the inflow of foreigners so long as real income was higher in the receiving country than in the source countries. Thus the flow would continue until real per capita incomes were equalized throughout the world. That would be at a level not much above that prevailing in the LDCs, where most of the world's population and labor force now live.

In practice, of course, those staggering consequences do not come about because purely and perfectly competitive labor markets are not permitted; instead all MDCs maintain barriers to immigration from abroad as well as various kinds of interference with competition in labor markets at home. These restrictions, amounting to institutional controls over employment and pay, maintain the present wage levels; that is, they "protect labor standards". This interpretation is consistent with the remarkable finding that when foreign workers do enter an MDC and obtain a job, their pay rate is seldom below that of adjacent native workers doing the same job.[18] The chief exception may be some all –immigrant–labor firms, where wages apparently go down to the statutory minimum, if not below it, and distinctly below prevailing wages for that kind of work (e.g., in the "new sweat-shops" that have recently appeared in garment-making shops in New York and in Los Angeles, according to press reports).

LABOR DEMAND AND THE SUPPLY OF AMERICAN AND FOREIGN WORKERS

Standard case of increase in labor supply, from S_0 to S_1.

Wage falls from w_0 to w_1;

total employment expands from q_0 to q_1;

American employment shrinks from q_0 to q_{1Am};

foreign workers enter in quantity $q_1 - q_{1Am}$.

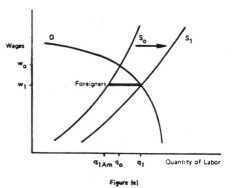

Figure (a)

Here the supply of unskilled foreigners for low-level jobs is "unlimited" at a "subsistence" wage w_2 which is below w_1.

Accordingly, total $q_2 >$ total q_1, but $q_{2Am} < q_{1Am}$.

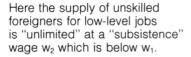

Here many Americans refuse to work at the prevailing wage w_0

for low-level jobs, causing shift of S_0 to S'_0; foreigners enter at that prevailing wage, preventing a wage rise above w_0,

and also preventing a corresponding reduction in total employment q_0 in this level of jobs;

but q_{3Am} often may be $< q_{2Am}$ in these jobs.

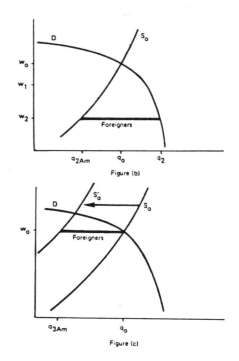

Figure (c)

Another qualification is that the inflow of foreigners into the labor force may tend to hold back desired and expected rises in pay rates; and incidentally may have contributed to the remarkably low rate of inflation in the U.S. during recent years. But foreigners at present volumes of net inflow do not usually—at least, not in most of the large establishments—tend to "undermine" or "depress" the existing wages and working conditions by the alleged tendency to "work for less pay."

Indeed, there is some indication—as noted above in regard to labor "needs" and "vacancies", and represented in part (c) of the diagram herewith—that foreign workers, at present volumes of net inflow, serve largely to replace natives, rather than displace them.[19] These natives are leaving various low–level occupations (or low–level segments of skilled occupations) because of preferable alternatives open to them (whether these are superior jobs or are other sources of support). Thus, immigration and the labor market may be adjusting the supply to the demand for labor in particular occupations—not perfectly, but closely enough to avoid major changes in vacancies and in wages. Further, immigrants seem to be prolonging the survival of some declining industries.

Besides the labor market impact and adjustment, immigration brings other stresses and alleged costs, both material effects and intangible ones. In the United States, foreigners entering currently —mostly Hispanics, Caribbean blacks, and Asians—tend to be quite alien in appearance and behavior from most of the native citizens and even from their ethnic predecessors, among whom they may settle. Of course, in northwestern Europe, where the native populations are much more homogeneous, the cultural conflicts with aliens from Mediterranean LDCs are still more acute. Where a large ethnic element is illegal, fears arise as to the maintenance of law and order, and these fears may extend blindly to look–alike aliens who have been admitted in entirely legal ways. Certain native institutions such as labor unions tend to be particularly fearful of the impact of foreign workers, who are inclined to be servile toward employers and docile before the authorities, especially in the case of the illegals who fear being denounced to the immigration agencies. On the other hand, some labor unions—particularly locals at the grassroots level—have found that even illegals can be enrolled as full dues-paying members, and they are actively proceeding to do so.

The most specific and pervasive charge as to the costs of foreign workers concerns their use of social services, supposedly without paying for them. There is an alleged scramble for limited supplies of low–rent housing, public schools, public hospitals, etc.; and a supposition that foreigners do not pay fees or taxes.

The facts here are in sharp dispute at the present time, largely because no adequate studies have been conducted. Available information indicates that the legal immigrants use social facilities and pay fees and taxes in about the same way as do comparable segments of the native population. However, the segments that are comparable here are mostly low-income persons, who in our society regularly receive substantial benefits in excess of their tax-payments. The legal immigrants receive about the same treatment as citizens.

As for the illegal immigrants, being mostly able-bodied young adults, they have much lower need or inclination to use public social services—except for hospitals in case of emergency, and except for children's schools in a few localities (some highly publicized instances in Texas). At the same time, the illegals do pay sales taxes, excise taxes, property taxes (as included in rents), and—when they are registered on bogus documents—they make income tax reports and they pay Social Security charges (although few will ever collect any Social Security benefits).[20]

In terms of settlement patterns, foreigners tend toward local concentrations that can be burdensome on inelastic supplies of housing and public facilities, especially in the older and non –expanding cities and towns. However, this may be only an argument for intergovernmental transfer payments to the localities from the national government, whose policy permits such inflows (the Simpson/Mazzoli immigration bill has proposed to make just such payments).

Finally, temporary workers admitted into the U.S. under the H–2 program do not bring dependents. Accordingly they do not make heavy use of social facilities here, and are not desperate to remain in this country permanently. Thus in the U.S., the social conflicts attending temporary foreign workers are minor compared to those in western Europe, where the guest workers have been allowed to bring in their dependents. Clearly there is need here to integrate immigration policy with welfare policy.

Effects of Emigration

The outflow of persons, who are partly professional and technical personnel (PTK) and partly unskilled mass laborers (UML), raises questions of economic and social effects in the countries of emigration as far-ranging as the effects of immigration into the receiving countries. However, the actual effects may be quite different, as the emigration nowadays flows mostly out of LDCs, characterized by surplus labor in most cases, whereas immigration flows mostly into MDCs which in most cases have relative scarcity of labor and intend to remain so.

Seeking a comprehensive and balanced list of the effects of emigration, we proceed in parallel with the taxonomy presented on a previous page for immigration effects.

IN COUNTRY OF EMIGRATION

Decrements/Increments	Benefits or Offsets
1) Reduction of population	Relief of population pressure, in some degree.
2) Reduction of labor force	Relief of unemployment and under–employment, in some degree; Possible scarcity of PTK—if not still surplus.
3) Wage effects	Little or no effect on wages, under conditions of unemployment and underemployment (since emigration does not usually drain those pools).
4) Reduction of consumption and retail sales	Relief of pressures on available goods and services, alleviating shortages and inflationary trends to some extent.
5) Reduced usage of social facilities	Relief of pressures and shortages, to some extent.
6) Receipt of emigrants' remittances, in foreign exchange	Aid to balance of international payments; increase in consumption and investment demand an purchasing power.
7) Return of some emigrants	Social disturbances, local inflationary pressures in short run, new entrepreneurship and productive skills.
8) Promotion/discouragement of economic modernization and development	Effects under 2, 3, 4, 6, 7 above; possible disincentives to national drive.

The economic and social effects of emigration, paralleling those of immigration, depend very much on the magnitudes and types of persons who move, and on the indirect and elusive consequences as well as the direct impacts. Debates in recent years have related mainly to the less-developed countries, whence the main emigration comes nowadays, and have concerned the two main groups of emigrants: the skilled and professional/technical workers (mostly covered under "PTK" in the U.S. Immigration Service's usage), and the unskilled mass laborers (whom we have designated "UML"). The conventional wisdom used to be that the PTK emigration was a "brain drain," namely a severe loss to LDCs, which were assumed, almost by definition, to have a shortage of skilled personnel. In contrast, in the same conventional wisdom, the UML emigration was almost always treated as a benefit—relieving overpopulation and unrest, securing jobs abroad, earning larger incomes in foreign exchange, and remitting a large part to the home family and country. Recently, however, both of those propositions have been reexamined and in part rebutted.

Examination of the alleged "brain drain" has focussed on the actual magnitude of the PTK outflows relative to the stock in the sending country, and further as to the country's "needs" for PTK (of the various types) and its "capacity to absorb" a PTK outflow of the actual or slightly enlarged magnitude. The findings amount to a demonstration that, in the chief countries of emigration, the PTK stock is in surplus (paralleling the surplus of UML); and accordingly, the current outflows from that stock are essentially an "overflow" which, in most countries, is not diminishing that stock (indeed, the outflows usually do not even offset the whole annual increment from the training schools.)[21] The fact is that since the last years of the 1960s, most of the LDCs that send out many PTKs have trained such large numbers of engineers, accountants, economists, nurses, doctors, and the like, as to exceed the practical needs of their country, as determined by the supply of cooperating inputs and the total purchasing power of the people and their government for those services. It is relatively low–cost in many LDCs to set up training programs for PTK, and to attract multitudes of students by publicizing high rates of return to education.[22] However, that publicity does not report the high and rising rates of unemployment of the PTK as their stock enlarges without limit. Indeed, in the Philippines, training schools for nurses and some other professionals are frankly "intended for the export market." Accordingly, in those places such personnel have a marginal productivity approaching zero, and their emigration has little or no effect on the output or development of their home country. Conversely, we find that LDCs that really need and use their PTK—providing them with opportunities for professional work and national service even if their salaries are below those in MDCs—do not lose many of them!

While those empirical and analytic studies of the emigration of PTK from LDCs have much diminished the clamor over "the brain drain" in the United Nations and some other circles, a new argument is arising in regard to the other main category, the UML emigration. Here it is charged that their outflow raises wages in the home country and thereby reduces employment and perhaps output; and that their remittances and returns home are variously wasteful, inflationary, disruptive, and non-developmental.[23]

This new attack on emigration is a curious mixture of a priori assumptions that dismiss the facts, and micro–analyses that miss the macro–phenomena here. First, to charge that UML emigration raises wages generally in that country is to deny the basic conditions of surplus labor in LDCs. The fact is that the emigration from most countries is, alas, far too small to drain off that surplus. For example, according to calculations in the World Bank's *World Development Report 1984*: "if 700,000 immigrants a year were admitted to the major host countries up to the year 2000, and all came from low–income countries, less than 2 percent of the projected growth in population in the low-income countries between 1982 and 2000 would have emigrated."

Even if we double those figures to allow for much larger actual world–wide migration nowadays,[24] the relief of population pressure by emigration amounts to only 4 percent of the expected *growth* in population, and does nothing to reduce the existing *arrears* of overpopulation! Thus, aside from some exceptional case, the overall surplus of population and labor in LDCs will not be reduced appreciably by emigration. The intramarginal reduction in labor supply will have little or no effect on wages in those countries.

In these considerations, LDCs must be carefully distinguished from semi–industrialized countries of emigration like Yugoslavia, whose experience with increasing scarcity of labor is overemphasized in the recent literature (see note 23). Likewise, if emigration does cause shortages of labor in particular industries and occupations—as is sometimes reported, for example, in Jamaica —a little time and expense must be allowed for adjustments via training and re-allocation.

Furthermore, it should be noted that any rise in wages attributable to emigration is a benefit for the people of LDCs directly in terms of lifting their level of living and welfare, mainly by raising their earnings out of the value–added, especially in export goods. To be sure, a quite large wage rise may discourage foreign and domestic investment in economic development in those countries (as observed recently in Singapore, as economic development in that small city-state drained the pool of local labor). However, in truly overpopulated large countries, the process of marginal emigration is unlikely to do more than to push wages up a little above the subsistence level.

In the second line of attack on emigration, to charge that remittances and repatriated savings only increase consumer imports at the expense of local producers is to ignore the facts that the funds from abroad are a net increment to the home economy, and that the propensity to import out of such funds is only fractional; also that the total value of imports will not become equal to the accrued foreign exchange unless there is indeed a powerful expansionary and developmental multiplier at work locally, stimulated by the funds from abroad.

Third, to complain that individual returnees do not seem to perform much investment is—even if it were true, which is denied by numerous reports—to ignore indirect investment by the whole economy. For example, purchases of land by returnees simply transfers the funds to the sellers, who then perform either additional consumption, direct investment, or deposits into the banking system. Indeed, all the foreign earnings flow into the banking system (in exchanges—at home or abroad—for local spendable currency), and add to the base for bank loans. Furthermore, all these financial flows increase the home government's tax base (sales taxes, property taxes, etc.), enlarging the government's spending power. Finally, to charge that the local governments are not formally channeling the foreign funds into development is to fall into the error of "misplaced concreteness," since all enlargement of the resources of the economy and its government go to cope with the country's economic problems, in which must be included consumption needs, imports, debt service, public services, as well as developmental projects and foreigners' direct investments, in whatever proportions seem most feasible and beneficial. For commentators to rely on micro–economics, in the face of these macro–phenomena, is to mislead oneself as well as one's audience.

Many accounts of emigration effects really expect too much in benefits—large, quick, and automatic benefits. When disappointed with the shortrun outcome, some call the process a "failure" or even "harmful," instead of settling for some net gains as better than none.

Striking a Net Balance on Migration

The patterns of benefit/cost outcomes of international migration, as explored in the preceding pages, may now be summarized for the two main groups of countries and the two main types of migrants:

a.   MDCs receiving immigrants nowadays generally gain from both high–level and low–level inflows, up to a certain volume (annual rate) which is determined in each case by national need and capacity–to–absorb–foreigners. A more flexible and adaptive control over the volume and types of immigration, and the conversion of illegal entries into legal admissions, including the safeguarded use of temporary foreign workers, would tend to raise the gains and minimize the burdens. Some particular groups and localities may always suffer some net adverse effects (externalities) from immigration, and deserve compensation out of the general gain.

b.   LDCs experiencing emigration nowadays also generally gain from both high–level and low–level outflows—except for a few places where PTK outflows come from meager stocks rather than the more usual surplus seeking emigration, excepting a few cases where return flows are disruptive rather than beneficial. As all emigrants represent international transfer of human capital, nurtured and trained at various magnitudes of cost (and cost –advantage), their native lands deserve international compensatory payments, supplementary foreign aid, or other offsets, with extra compensation for some particularly hard–hit places of origin.

From these viewpoints, international migration in certain limited magnitudes is a positive–sum transaction for almost all parties, albeit in differing absolute and relative amounts. To facilitate these transactions, and more nearly equalize the net benefits, international migration should not be left entirely to unilateral controls, but should also be subject to multilateral agreements among nations.

Policy Implications

The analyses in this paper imply a new labor–market approach to immigration. This would seek to control total inflows according to the receiving country's labor needs and its capacity to absorb foreigners; and thereby to reduce conflicts with native–born workers, while filling job vacancies in firms and agencies. Such a policy would comprise:

a.   strong labor–force criteria for limiting admissions of all permanent-stay immigrants;

b.   development of the existing small H-2 program into a targeted Temporary Foreign Workers system, so as to fill low–level vacancies, in urban as well as rural jobs, in a legal way and thereby curtail unauthorized immigration;

c.   steps for upgrading the low–level stratum; and

d.   compensation for localities particularly impacted by immigration or emigration.

This four-fold set of proposals evolves from existing practices but goes far beyond the Simpson–Mazzoli bill that failed to pass the U.S. Congress in 1984. The present proposals are feasible to operate, low in cost, and socially acceptable.[25]

Overall Criteria for Authorized Migration

1.   *The joint problem of unemployment, vacancies, and immigration.* One of the major employment problems of MDCs in our time is the joint coexistence of a persistently high rate of unemployment, a wide array of unfilled jobs, and a very large volume of net immigration. The unemployment problem, arising from domestic and international influences upon the supply and demand of labor, is exacerbated by the largely uncontrolled, and indeed unparalleled, entries of foreigners into the labor force. At the same time, there are vacant jobs, not only at the highest level of skills (which are always in short supply), but also at the next–to –highest level in particular unattractive conditions, terms and locations (e.g., interns and residents in hospitals in poor or remote areas), and also in the low–level range of jobs which most American workers, even when unemployed, tend to reject, or to

do with low performance and high turnover. These coexistences amount to a disorderly labor market that can only be remedied by public policy.

The whole range of the required policies would go too far afield for the present paper, as it would include:

a. reformed macro–practices, to reduce the Federal deficit, bring down interest rates, and deflate the dollar;

b. adjusted industrial policies, to close down sunset industries while promoting sunrise sectors;

c. training and re-locating the particularly displaced, unskilled and maladjusted labor cohorts; etc.

The present paper concentrates on reforming immigration policies, within the larger context of institutions and programs to be reconstructed.

2. *Immigration is virtually uncontrolled at present.* The annual inflow of all foreigners for long stay in this country amounts, according to the best estimates, to about half of our annual growth in population and labor force. While it is an addition to our demographic stock of only one percent a year (net), the total of the "recently accumulated" stock of alien workers is almost exactly equal to our total unemployed. The impact is much heavier on particular localities and certain occupations, where immigrants are in some competition with Americans for jobs and social services. Offsetting these impacts are the cost–control, inflation –control, and even the survival of some industries (fruits and vegetables, the garment industry, cleaning services, etc.), plus their contributions to the variety and dynamism of our society.

The present system supposedly regulating immigration is in fact defective, and has nearly broken down, as regards the so-called "quotas" for authorized admissions, as well as regards the unauthorized border–crossers and visitor stay–ons. Probably the only alien-control systems that are functioning efficiently, and as intended, are the programs for temporary foreign workers (the H-2 and Exchange Visitor programs.)

3. *Policies to control authorized admissions.* Policies for authorized immigration should begin by putting all permanent –type admissions on a rational basis. The total numbers for each year should be governed by Labor Department surveys of the

American labor–market's "needs for workers" and the American society's "capacity to absorb foreigners," plus reviews of recent experience. One specific aid for measuring "needs" would be the construction of an Index of Vacancies (as done in several European countries); next best would be counts of Want Ads. Likewise, "capacity to absorb" can be indicated by counts of empty places in schools, hospitals, and dwelling units.

So far as additional admissions are approved in order to reunify families and to provide asylum for political and religious refugees, their numbers should either be limited to the country's needs and capacity to absorb; or else the admissions of workers per se should be curtailed to allow for the predictable labor–force participation by those admittedly family members and refugees.

As for the source countries, their national quotas—which at present are a uniform 20,000 per country—should be adaptable within the immigration grand total. Thus India, for example, would be allowed a suitably larger number than Jamaica or Hong Kong.

Policies to control unauthorized entries

1. *Four ways to control illegal entries.* We face a choice among four basic approaches:

a. a simple, absolute closure of the borders, using as much force as may be required, plus close scrutiny of all visitors to this country;

b. the Simpson–Mazzoli proposal for prohibiting firms to employ undocumented aliens, to be implemented with secure I.D. cards; or

c. an adapted Temporary Foreign workers program designed to preclude the jobs which currently attract undocumented entrants; or

d. a long–range program for the source countries, to reduce their emigration by promoting birth control, job creation, and general economic development.

Of these four approaches, the first is presumably rejected by most Americans, as amounting to a kind of "Berlin Wall" that is incompatible with democracy and humane values.

The much debated Simpson–Mazzoli proposals have been opposed on one side as probably ineffectual—in the light of European experience with sanctions on employers; and condemned on another side as tending to discrimination, and even as an invasion of privacy of all Americans.

The fourth approach seeking to remove the basic causes of emigration from less–developed countries, is admirable and indeed necessary for the long run; but it is very costly and slow to yield results. At this moment it is of little help, in view of the millions of "surplus labor" already born, and under–employed, and seeking escape from the poor countries.

2.   The best resort: an enlightened TFW program. Turning to the remaining approach, a suitable Temporary Foreign Workers (TFW) program can be built upon the existing H-2 and Exchange programs. It would admit specified numbers of aliens, without dependents, for specified work periods (up to one year usually, or at most three) in stipulated regions of this country and in stipulated occupations, urban as well as rural, and at least initially in a specified firm. Freedom for these workers to change jobs might be granted under several arrangements: frequent reporting, withholding of part of earnings until repatriation, linkage with the home government, or finally sanctions on employers.

This TFW program would offer to the aliens a system of secure entries with full civil rights, at officially supervised pay–scale and working conditions not below our national standards. The legitimate filling of jobs would discourage the present inflow via surreptitious, expensive, and risky channels, into insecure status here. American workers would be protected from unfair competition, mainly by illicit undercutting of our standards by the illegals. The source countries of the TFWs would receive their remittances, and later their return home with, in some cases, investible capital and usuable skills.

The exclusion of the TFW's dependents, which may seem harsh, is of course intended to diminish any impact on American social facilities, as well as to avoid the European difficulties with the repatriation of their guest–workers who had put down family roots. In our proposed TFW program, the worker would be separated from his family only for a year or so; and would be encouraged to make intermediate home visits; and would be obliged to make regular remittances to the dependents he has temporarily left behind.

Upgrading Jobs and Workers

It is sometimes charged that such a TFW program "tends to create a permanent under–class." However this charge ignores the actual rotation of foreign individuals in the program, and the provisions for maintaining national standards of work and pay in the receiving country.

More important, there is nothing in this program to block the up–grading of low–level jobs—whether by technologic advances, rationalization enlargement of scale, changing social values, or merely raising the statutory minima for wages and working conditions. While the availability of a low–cost labor force is sometimes said to discourage employers' interest in upgrading jobs, the prospect of extra profitability from any available improvements is usually a powerful stimulant; and of course innumerable jobs, formerly on a low level, have already been markedly upgraded, in the whole course of industrialization. Technologic improvements mostly depend on research and development, which can be promoted by fiscal incentives (especially tax credits) and by institutional adjustments (such as exempting colloborative research from anti–trust prohibitions). Finally, much can be learned from social practices in Japan, which gets its low–level work done acceptably by natives, plus Koreans who immigrated in earlier decades and with almost no immigration or illegal entries nowadays.

Compensation for Local Impacts

1. *In an MDC receiving immigration.* When a national or Federal immigration program imposes appreciable burdens on a particular locality, Federal compensation should be paid.

The impact of immigrants is easily exaggerated as to the receiving nations, inasmuch as they add only a tiny increment each year. However, the initial incidence is sometimes substantial for certain localities and occupations. According to recent studies (as discussed in the section on Capacity to Absorb Foreign workers), the legal immigrants use our social services to about the same degree as do natives in similar income and occupational classes, whereas the illegal entrants make little use of hospitals, schools, welfare programs and unemployment insurance—unless they bring in dependents and pass themselves off as legitimate residents.

Whether aliens' use of these facilities constitutes a real burden depends on whether these facilities locally are in scarce or in surplus supply. In the latter case—e.g., idle housing for which immigrants pay rent, or public schools operating below normal sized classes—the social costs of incremental usage are almost zero. However, in the case of scarce facilities, the user costs are appreciable; yet they are not the average, or per–capita, costs—as commonly reckoned—but are only the marginal or incremental costs, which are usually much less in already existing agencies. These marginal costs are the burden to be compensated by the national or Federal government, mostly as a form of inter –governmental transfers.

2.   *Compensation from receiving country to country of origin.* When emigration from an LDC into an MDC actually imposes appreciable burdens on the former, compensation should be paid by the latter.

However, most LDCs do not suffer such burdens, since most countries of emigration are characterized by a surplus of personnel—whether the emigration is from the professional or the mass-labor levels—and the "lost" marginal product of the emigrants is therefore close to zero, while the training and recruitment of substitutes for the emigrants is going on all the time. Furthermore, most LDCs are receiving remittances from the emigrants, repatriations bring back capital and skills in many instances, and foreign aid from MDCs.

It is therefore a rare LDC that is not already compensated, or over–compensated, for the alleged burdens of emigration. Yet, in the special case where the emigrating personnel were scarce, and showed positive marginal product that was sacrificed, a corresponding specific compensation should be paid, in one direct form or another.[26] At the same time, such an LDC might be expected to persuade its needed personnel to stay and work in the home country; or else use its foreign aid receipts to train replacements for the emigrants.

NOTES

1.   Regarding these judgements, see E.P. Reubens, "International Migration Models and Policies" *American Economic Review*, May 1983, especially pp. 178-180.

2.   For details of N/CA and A/O/M models, see E. P. Reubens, *Interpreting Migration*, Center for Latin American and Caribbean Studies, New York University, Occasional Paper No. 29, 1981.

3.   Our estimate of 4 million in 1978 for the stock of recently accumulated aliens working in the U.S. combines:

a.   accumulation of 1 million immigrant workers legally admitted during 1974-78 (admissions totaling 2.2 million persons, reduced by 25% for estimated return flows, and multiplied by a 60% labor–participation rate); plus

b.   the stock of admitted temporary workers, at about 120,000 (the average annual admissions, slightly enlarged for some stays beyond one year); and

c.   the stock of unauthorized resident workers, at about 3 million (derived from a Census staff assessment for 1978, *cit. inf.*, multiplied by a 75% labor–participation rate).

Our estimate for 1984, namely a stock of 8 million alien workers, is assembled from:

a.   accumulation of nearly 2 million immigrant workers legally admitted during 1979–84 (by calculation paralleling a. above); plus

b.   the stock of admitted temporary workers as in b. above); and

c.   the stock of unauthorized resident workers, at over 6 million, accumulated from annual net inflows of 600,000 a year (see fn. 14), during 1979-84, and added to the 3 million stock as of 1978.

The ratios used in the foregoing estimates are derived from agency interviews as well as published sources which include: L.F. Bouvier chapter in M. Kritz, ed., *U.S. Immigration and Refugee Policy* (Heath, 1983), p. 198; and B. Chiswick in W. Fellner, ed., *Contemporary Economic Problems* (American Enterprise Institute, 1980); and Siegel, Passell and Robinson, "Preliminary Review of Existing Studies of Illegal Residents in U.S." (Census Bureau staff paper, 1980: not an official report).

4.   *Cf.* M. Baily in *Brookings Review*, Fall 1983, p. 28, implying only 2 million shortfall; and P. Rones in *Monthly Labor Review*, Feb. 1984.

5.   Canada, Department of Employment and Immigration, *Immigration Statistics*, 1981, Table 2: and *Annual Report to Parliament*, Nov. 1983.

6.   Emigration estimates, and relative volume of net immigration, from Kritz, Keely and Tomasi, *Global Trends in Migration* (Center for

Migration Studies, 1981), pp. 199-201, citing Barrett and Taylor, *Population and Canada* (University of Toronto, 1977). *Cf.* population shares in Canada in 1981: Canadian–born 20.2 million, Foreign–born 3.8 million (*Immigration Statistics*, Table 1).
Relative to unemployment in Canada, which ran between 800,000 and 900,000 during 1977-81, but jumped to 1,300,000 in 1982, the next immigration of 70,000 a year in the 1970s, and 50,000 a year in the 1980s, was quite small in the range of 8% - 4% (unemployment data from *Monthly Labor Review*, Jan. 1984, Table 1, p. 45).

7.   Data on Western Europe from W.R. Bohning, *Studies in International Migration* (London: Macmillian, 1984), and from *OECD Observer*, March 1979, May 1980, and July 1984.

8.   See U.S. Select Commission on Immigration and Refugee Policy, *Staff Report* (Washington, D.C., 1981) especially chapter 9, summarizing studies by North and Houston (1976), Cornelius (1977), and others.

9.   *Immigration Statistics, cit. sup.,* Table 1. Canada also has a small program of "temporary employment visas," used to fill short–term vacancies, both agricultural and non–agricultural, and generally without provision for dependents.

10.   For details, see E.P. Reubens, "Some Dimensions of Professional Immigration" in J.N. Bhagwati, ed., *The Brain Drain and Taxation,* Vol II, (North Holland Publ. Co., 1976), Appendix 11.2.

11.   *Ibid.,* pp. 222-5; See also Stevens and Vermeulen, *Foreign Trained Physicians and American Medicine* (H.E.W. Department, Washington, 1972).

12.   See E.P. Reubens, "The New Brain Drain from Developing Countries" in R.L. Leiter, ed., *Costs and Benefits of Education* (G.K. Hall, 1975) pp. 192-3; and in some dimensions . . . " *cit, sup.,* pp. 227-8, 241-2.

13.   For the statistical record in West Germany and the cited explanation, see Bohning (1984: *cit. sup.*), p. 75 and Tables 5.3 and 5.4. For comparison with the U.S. experience, see E.P. Reubens, *Temporary Admission of Foreign Workers,* National Commission for Employment Policy, Special Report No. 34 (Washington: G.P.O. 1979).

14.   I.N.S. reported apprehension figure is 1 million annually, or about 600,000 net of duplicate reporting: to this we apply the low end of the Border Patrol's estimates of the evasion rate (i.e., 2 evaders per apprehended individual, or 1.2 per gross apprehension), and then apply an 80% rate of labor-force participation (slightly above the resident illegals rate), to arrive at 960,000 illegal worker entries: then deduction for short stays yields approximately 600,000, which may be interpreted, as "full–year equivalent workers" illegally entering each year surreptitiously. This figure may be enlarged by aliens entering on Visitor Visas and covertly overstaying.

15. See Wool and Phillips, *The Labor Supply for Lower-level Occupations* (National Planning Assn., 1975); also M. Wachter, *The Labor Market and Immigration: Outlook for the 1980s* (University of Pennsylvania, Feb. 1979); and the projections of labor demand and supply in *Monthly Labor Review*, Nov. 1983, and in *N.Y. Times* section "Careers '85", Nov. 14. 1984.

16. The latest attack on the reported "need for alien workers" is a dire warning to the employers against becoming "dependent on illegal alien labor" or even dependent on legal aliens: see M. Teitelbaum, *Immigration, Refugees and American Business*, National Chamber of Commerce Foundation, 1984, and likewise P. Martin, "Labor Intensive Agriculture," in *Scientific American*, Oct. 1983. Each writer seems to believe that industries which rely on aliens become or remain "under–capitalized" and therefore are bound to have low productivity. They specifically overlook the character of the product and the available technology in those industries, which cannot pay higher real wages per worker until some revolution in technology comes forward (and incidentally then reduces employment per unit of product).

17. See E.P. Reubens, "Low–Level Work in Japan Without Foreign Workers", *International Migration Review* vol. 15, No. 4, Jan. 1982; reprinted as monography by The Environmental Fund, Washington, Dec. 1982.

18. See D. North and M. Houstoun, *Characteristics and Role of Illegal Aliens in the U.S. Labor Market* (Linton & Co., 1976), pp. 128-130. Even opponents of foreign worker programs recognize that "most illegal immigrants do receive at least the Federal minimum wage and many receive much more" (V. Briggs, in *"The Border That Joins,"* Brown and Shue, eds., Littlefield, 1982). A similar statement, based on field work in northern New Jersey, appears in a paper given by D. Papademetriou and N. DiMarzio at the APSA meeting, August 1984, p. 14 and Table 4. Additional confirmation is found in NACLA, *Report on the Americas* vol. XII, No. 6, Nov-Dec. 1979, pp. 18-19.

19. Some social scientists, implicitly adopting a kind of "jobs fund" notion, assume that entry of immigrant workers must displace native workers either one-for-one or in some high ratio: e.g., Donald Huddle, Rice University, assumes in a recent study that displacement is 3:2 (N.Y. Times, Jan. 4, 1984). Other social scientists such as Julian Simon, Illinois and Maryland Universities (unpublished paper, 1984 draft) claim that displacement is very small utilizing rather inadequate data and measurements, they find that changes in unemployment rates among several cities are not correlated with their inflows of immigrants. Both contending parties tend to rely on neo–classical market axioms that ignore segmented labor markets and non–competing groups of workers. T. Muller, in paper given at APSA meeting, August 1984, using statistical data on

earnings, unemployment, and migration in California, in relation to structured labor markets, found very small economic effects from immigration, even from illegal immigration.

As regards short–run (business cycle) fluctuations of economic conditions in the countries of immigration, it is commonly supposed that migrants adjust by delaying or reducing their movements during recessions there. However, U.S. experience in recent years does not support the supposed short–run correlation. In terms of our A/O/M model of migration causation, the aspirations and mobility of migrants are matters of long–run rising trends, and even the differentials in opportunities are matters of secular disparities not much altered by short–run fluctuations in either the sending or the receiving country.

20.   Several sample studies, on the services used and the payments made by illegals in the U.S., are summarized in the chapter by D. North in Kritz, ed., U.S. Immigration (cit. sup.). The consensus is that while legal immigrants use public services and pay taxes did about the "average" rate of the corresponding U.S. population, the Illegals' use of the services is "below average" (although not zero), while their tax payments came close to the average for their economic level.

A huge net social burden was charged to illegals—nearly $6 billion a year, net of taxes paid by them—in a paper by an I.N.S. office in California, and endorsed by R. Conner of FAIR in a letter in N.Y. Times, Dec. 13, 1983; (cit. sup.). All three of these assume heavy unemployment compensation to American workers who are allegedly displaced by foreign workers in very high ratios and are not absorbed elsewhere without justifying these assumptions.

Other estimates were collected in a brochure entitled "Illegal Aliens —A 'Free Lunch' Myth", issued by FAIR in early 1984, and termed "startling" and "shocking". Actually, however, they are mostly unrepresentative extreme cases, and are commonly presented as absolute numbers (benefitted persons and/or dollars of benefits) without any evaluative reference or standard of judgement (particularly without reference to the low-income class of these persons).

An intensive, though not very comprehensive, study was done in 1982-83 by S. Weintraub and G. Cardenas in the State of Texas (presented at the American Political Science Association in August 1984). It was found that the State's public services provided to Illegals cost less than the taxes they paid to the State; but for six individual cities in Texas, the reverse was true. Unfortunately, this study minimized the taxes collected (especially omitting property taxes paid in rent bills); and also omitted all unemployment compensation payments; and did not quantify its distinction between "transient illegals" who use few public services, and "resident illegals" living as a family with dependents.

Perhaps the best study to date is by Thomas Muller, The Fourth Wave (Washington: The Urban Institute, 1984), which states (p. 21) that in California the social–services costs of recent Mexican immigrants (the majority being undocumented) exceed the taxes they pay by about $2,000 a year per household; but also that this "deficit" is about the same as for American families with similarly low incomes and large numbers of children.

21.   See G. Baldwin, "Brain Drain or Overflow," *Foreign Affairs*, Jan. 1970; E.P. Reubens, "The New Brain Drain from Developing Countries" in R.L. Leiter, ed., *Costs and Benefits of Education* (G.K. Hall, 1975), pp. 193-204; UNESCO, *The Migration of Talent* (17 C/58, Oct. 1972); and Colombo Plan Bureau, *Special Topic; Brain Drain* (New Delhi, 1972).

22.   See Blaug, Layard, and Woodhall, *The Causes of Graduate Unemployment in India* (London: Penguin, 1969); India, Council of Scientific and Industrial Research, *Technical Manpower*, April 1972; M.L. Gupta, "Outflow of High Level Manpower from the Phillipines," *International Labor Review*, Feb. 1973; N.Y. Times, "Kenya Students Spending Years Looking for Jobs," Jan. 22, 1978.

23.   See for example the papers by A.P. Maingot and by E. Thomas –Hope given at the Conference on Migration and Development in the Caribbean at Aspen Institute, MD., in Sept. 1984; T. McCoy at session on International Migration at American Political Science Assn. (APSA) meeting in Washington, D.C. in Aug. 1984; D. Papademetriou at APSA meeting in Sept. 1982; H. Rubenstein in *Human Organization*, Winter 1983; chapter on "Emigration from the Mediterranean Basin" in Bohning (1984, *cit. sup.*); etc. Most of these treatments are very impassioned and in a "rush to policy," but are poorly documented and imperfectly argued. The Bohning discussion, which aims at balanced and factual demonstration, concedes *passim* some large benefits to LDCs from emigration, remittances, and returns.

24.   An estimate of total international migration nowadays begins with U.S. legal admissions of about 600,000 a year in the 1980s, plus other MDC admissions, for a total of about 800,000 in this category; to which we add net undocumented entries, worldwide, at roughly 700,000 a year; arriving at a total of about 1,500,000 annually.

25.   These recommendations on migration policy, for both MDCs and LDCs, in slightly different form were presented in the writer's testimony before the Select Commission on Immigration and Refugee Policy (*U.S. Immigration Policy and the National Interest, Staff Report*, Washington: G.P.O., 1981); and are also discussed more fully in E.P. Reubens, *The Challenge of the New International Economic Order*, Chapter on "International Migration in North South Relations" (Boulder, CO., Westview Press, 1981).

26.   The form and channel of compensation to LDC source countries might be a special tax on the income of the individual emigrant, collected by the government where he works, and transmitted to the government of the nation that he left—as sketched by J.N. Bhagwati in the volume *cit.*

sup. (fn. 10), and elsewhere. Alternatively and more easily, the compensation might be an appropriate increase in bilateral foreign aid, taken from general tax revenues derived from the national income, which presumably includes the emigrant's economic contribution in the MDC—as outlined in E.P. Reubens, *The Challenge of the New International Economic Order,* cit. sup., p. 248.

CHAPTER 2

KOREANS IN AMERICA: RECENT MIGRATION FROM SOUTH KOREA TO THE UNITED STATES

P. W. Kuznets

Recent mass migration, particularly to newly expanding labor markets in the Middle East or from war and revolution in countries like Cuba and Vietnam, has renewed interest in the phenomenon of international migration. The basic questions associated with this migration have to do with who migrates, why they migrate, and what the impact of their migration is on sending and receiving countries. Of particular interest, perhaps, is the sort of migration that is inspired neither by obvious causes such as flight from hostile regimes nor by the relatively high wages offered to transient workers but, rather, follows from a decision to leave familiar surroundings in order to begin a new life in another country. Reasons for leaving are not only less obvious in this instance, but so are the attractions of migration since the psychic and other costs would seem to be much higher when the move is regarded as permanent rather than temporary.

Other costs of migration beside psychic costs are travel costs and the cost of support while searching for a job. Benefits, in turn, should include the appropriately discounted stream of extra income that is expected to result from higher earnings in the receiving country. The costs and benefits which count in the decision to migrate are expected rather than actual costs and benefits so that actual net benefits may prove to be more or less than anticipated. Since psychic costs of separation persist, unlike travel and settling-in costs, and these are particularly difficult to anticipate, underestimates may explain the phenomenon of return migration. Other non–economic factors may explain the phenomenon of return migration. Other non–economic factors besides psychic costs that should play a part in the decision to migrate include better access to education and opportunity for rejoining friends and family, though these can be viewed in economic terms as reducing costs. While the decision to migrate reflects supply side considerations, actual migration is limited by quotas, visa limitations, and the other demand side restrictions imposed on immigrants by receiving countries. The Immigration Act of 1965, for example, began the phasing out of the national–origins quota system in the United States and had a lot to do with the subsequent increase in immigration from countries in the Eastern Hemisphere.

The economic impact of migration depends on perspective and on whether factor markets are or are not imperfect. Perspective varies according to whether one includes citizens who have migrated as well as those who remain in assessing economic effects (national perspective) or whether one considers only the effects on those who remain (domestic perspective). The broadest perspective—the global perspective—weighs effects on all persons in both sending and receiving countries. The literature has focused primarily on the effects of brain drain (migration of high–level manpower) on output and welfare in the sending country from the domestic point of view. If migration is significant, productivity of remaining workers will rise, that of cooperating factors (land and capital) will fall and, to the extent that producer surplus is lost, labor's gain will not fully offset capitalist's losses. This conclusion has to be modified, however, when there are market imperfections. Where unemployment exists, for example, emigration may not reduce output, nor may immigration increase it. Also, to the extent that education is subsidized, and supported by taxes on the higher incomes of the educated, the process of intergenerational transfer may be short

circuited by the departure of professionals who have received
their education but who have yet to pay for the next generation's education. Other considerations, such as remittances
by emigrants or the possibility that higher education of high–
level manpower has been in the receiving rather than in
the sending country, complicate the analysis further. These
considerations are too complex for me to do justice to here,
but one consequence of this complexity seems clear. While
there is substantial theoretical literature on the economic
effects of emigration, very little has been done to measure
such effects.[1]

Of the three basic questions, that of who migrates is simplest to
answer. Answers to this question also suggest something about
why people migrate. Cost–benefit considerations, in addition,
provide clues on what might be found. Travel and job search
costs, for example, should deter the rich from migrating less than
the poor, while benefits should be greater where wage differentials between sending and receiving countries are larger and for
the young who can anticipate a longer earning life than older
persons. Economic effects should be most difficult to assess, and
are likely to be relatively greater for small sending countries than
for large receiving ones. The purpose of this paper is to essay
answers to these questions for recent migration from South Korea
(hereafter, simply "Korea") to the United States. This particular
stream of international migrants should prove more revealing of
answers than most. Korean migration appears to be voluntary
rather than forced and, insofar as permanence can be ascertained,
to be permanent rather than temporary. (Permanence is at issue
until death, but high naturalization rates among Korean emigrants
indicate intent to stay in the U.S.)[2] Also, Korean censuses provide
unusually good data on demographic and economic characteristics of Koreans. These can now be supplemented with
information by detailed racial background from the 1970
and 1980 U.S. population censuses. In addition, this information and annual data on migrants published by the U.S.
Immigration and Naturalization Service (INS) show that
Koreans were among the major Asian migrant groups in the
1970s, and that the rate of increase in numbers of foreign born
Koreans from 1970 to 1980 was significantly higher than that
of other major Asian emigrant groups for which 1970 data
are available. Korean migration to the United States, in short,
has increased to the point that it is now significant in its own
right.

Migrants and Their Reasons for Migrating

The first Koreans who came to what is now the United States were the seven thousand laborers that left Korea in 1902 to 1905 to work on the sugar plantations in the Hawaiian Islands. Such immigration, covered under a "Treaty of Amity and Commerce" signed by the two countries in 1882, was inspired by difficult conditions in Korea after the Sino–Japanese War (1894 to 1895) when the peninsula became a battleground and many Koreans were uprooted from their homes, and by the drought of 1901. Also, the Hawaiian planters were eager to use Koreans in place of Japanese workers who were demanding higher wages and better working conditions. Emigration from Korea slowed after 1905 when the Japanese tightened their hold on the country after the Russo–Japanese War and banned emigration, probably to protect the Japanese working in Hawaii.[3] Except for several thousand "picture brides," students, intellectuals, and political exiles, there was no emigration from Korea to the United States until after Korea was liberated from Japanese rule at the end of World War II. During the quarter of a century from the end of World War II to 1970, when detailed race (ethnic) categories were first employed in a U.S. census, migration must have been very limited. There were fewer than 71 thousand Koreans in the United States, and of these, only 38 thousand were foreign born (see Table 1).[4]

By 1980, the second census to include information by detailed race, the number of Koreans had quintupled to 357 thousand so that Koreans were then—along with the Japanese, Chinese, Filipinos, Indians, and Vietnamese—among the major Asian immigrant groups. One source of this growth was the increase in overall U.S. immigration levels from an annual average of 347 thousand in 1966 to 1969 (excluding Cuban refugees) to 531 thousand in 1978 to 1980. This increase was sufficient to raise the proportion of foreign born in the United States from 4.7 percent in 1970 to 6.2 percent in 1980 (Table 1), and possibly higher to the extent that the census data do not record the presence of illegal immigrants. Other sources were the Immigration Act of 1965, which eliminated national–origins quotas by mid–1968, and the exemption of families of U.S. citizens from visa ceilings. In addition, a preference system favoring professionals resulted in Asia replacing Europe as the main source of migrants stating an occupation.[5] While elimination of national–origins quotas and the new preference system have favored Asians in general, they do not account for the comparatively rapid growth in Korean emigration to the

United States. One reason for this above average increase is that large percentage growth is more likely to occur from small than from large bases. This is suggested by comparing the 1970 to 1980 percentage increases for foreign–born Koreans, Japanese and Chinese in the United States with the 1970 levels, both given in Table 1. Similar calculations for Filipinos and Indians, other major immigrant groups not shown in Table 1, tend to confirm this, as the increase among Indians (small base) was much larger than that for Filipinos (large base). Other possible reasons for the particularly large expansion of Korean emigration to the United States can be found by examining the immigration status, demographic, and economic characteristics of Korean emigrants.

The two major categories of immigrants listed in INS statistics include the occupational preference category, divided among occupational sub-categories, and others labeled as "housewives, children, and no occupation reported." The 1978 figures for these categories, which seem to be representative of other years during the 1970s, are given for Korean immigrants, all immigrants and the U.S. population at large (1980) in Table 2. Several differences are immediately apparent when comparing Korean immigrants, all immigrants, and the U.S. population. First, proportionately more Korean immigrants are professionals and fewer are laborers and farmers than are found among other immigrant groups or in the U.S. aggregate. Overall, there are more laborers and farmers among immigrants and fewer clerical and sales workers than in the U.S. totals; which suggests that recent immigrants who maintain their occupation enter at the bottom of the occupational hierarchy but, because of assimilation problems, are not selected if jobs with their training require contact with the public. Second, the proportion of housewives, children, and those without an occupation reported is much higher for Koreans than for the other two groups. The distribution of Korean immigrants by age and sex therefore seems worth examining to see who these dependents are.

Age distributions and sex ratios (number of males per 100 females) for Korean immigrants and all immigrants (1978) and for the U.S. population as a whole (1980) are presented in Table 3. The table shows the immigrants' relative youth; over 60 percent are under 30, compared with 50 percent for the United States, while the population share of those over age 60 in the United States is about three times as large as that among the immigrants. This reflects both the young age distributions among sending countries (in 1980, two of every three Koreans were under 30) and

THE ECONOMICS OF MASS MIGRATION

TABLE 1
KOREANS, JAPANESE, AND CHINESE IN THE UNITED STATES: 1970 AND 1980

	Koreans	Japanese	Chinese	Total Population (000s)
1970				
A. Total	70,598	588,324	431,583	203,212
B. Foreign-born	38,145	122,500	204,232	9,619
% Foreign-born	54.0	20.8	47.3	4.7
1980				
C. Total	357,393	716,331	812,178	226,546
D. Foreign-born	292,573	203,338	514,389	14,080
% Foreign-born	81.9	28.4	63.3	6.2
Increase,				
Foreign-born	254,428	80,838	310,157	4,461
C ÷ A (%)	506.2	121.8	188.2	111.5
D ÷ B (%)	767.0	166.0	251.9	146.4

SOURCES: U.S. Department of Commerce, Bureau of the Census, *1970 Census of Population Subject Report*, PC(2)-1G; *1980 Census of Population*, Part 1, U.S. Summary (PC80-1-D1-A).

TABLE 2
OCCUPATIONAL DISTRIBUTION OF KOREAN
IMMIGRANTS, ALL IMMIGRANTS, AND THE U.S.
POPULATION AT LARGE: 1978

Occupation	Korean Immigrants Number	%	All Immigrants Number	%	U.S. (000s)[2] Number	%
Prof., Tech., Managerial	3,468	48.0	69,806	28.0	25,133	25.7
Clerical and Sales	1,219	16.8	33,847	13.6	26,612	27.3
Craftsmen and Operators	1,729	23.9	75,067	30.2	26,086	26.7
Laborers and Farmers	301	4.2	34,526	13.9	7,196	7.4
Service (incl. domestics)	515	7.1	35,517	14.3	12,629	12.9
Subtotal[1]	7,232	100.0	248,763	100.0	97,639	100.0
Housewives, children, no occupation reported	22,056	75.3	352,679	58.6	128,907	56.9
Total	29,288	100.0	601,442	100.0	226,546	100.0

[1] Percentage distribution of occupational subcategories.

[2] Figures for 1980, not 1978, employed only.

Sources: INS, *1978 Statistical Yearbook of the Immigration and Naturalization Service*, p. 17. For fiscal year ending September 30.

Bureau of the Census, *1980 Census of Population*, General Social and Economic Characteristics, U.S. Summary (PC80-1-C1).

the makeup of the immigrants, who include even more young and fewer older persons than the populations from which they are drawn. Sex ratios are not too different for most Koreans, all –immigrant, and U.S. age groups with the notable exception of those aged 0–5 and 20–29, where females greatly outnumber males. The unusually large number and high proportion of females among the 0–5 age group for Korean immigrants results from adoption by Americans of Korean orphans. The low sex ratio may result either from Korean reluctance to give up boys for adoption or an American preference for adopting girls rather than boys. The INS shows that there have been 5 to 6 thousand orphans among the immigrants to the United States each year from 1976 to 1980, and of these, more than half come from Korea. Of the 4,155 Korean immigrants to the United States aged 0–5 in 1978, for example, 3,045 were orphans. The unusually high proportion of women among the 20–29 age group, in turn, can be explained by the presence of 40 thousand or more U.S. troops in Korea since the end of the Korean War in 1953, many of whom have married Korean women.[6]

Education, occupation, location, and other social and economic characteristics that seem likely to influence economic performance are of particular interest here. Economic performance of recent Korean immigrants, as measured by household or family income, may also be affected by difficulties with the new language, nontransferability of their education, or discrimination against immigrants in the workplace. While we have no information on discrimination or on assimilation problems, we can use the 1980 U.S. Census of Population to analyze the social and economic characteristics that are likely to influence income. Causal relations are sometimes ambiguous so that high income may require urban residence, for instance, rather than urban residence contributing to high income, but the usual assumption is adopted that income is the dependent rather than the explanatory variable.[7] The 1980 Census data cover all Koreans in the United States, a group that is not ideal for present purposes because it includes native as well as foreign born, and because the foreign born include non–immigrants as well as immigrants. This group, however, is the closest that one can get to Korean immigrants, the population of interest. It should be a reasonable proxy for the immigrants because over 80 percent of the group are foreign born and, with heavy recent immigration, nearly all foreign born should be immigrants.

Household and family income rather than individual income are examined because households and families are the principal

TABLE 3
AGE AND SEX DISTRIBUTIONS: KOREAN
IMMIGRANTS, ALL IMMIGRANTS, AND THE U.S.
POPULATION AT LARGE: 1978

Age Group	Korean Immigrants %	Sex Ratio[1]	All Immigrants %	Sex Ratio[1]	U.S. (000s)[2] %	Sex Ratio[1]
Under 5	14.2	61	5.9	98	7.2	105
5–9	10.4	98	8.6	106	7.4	105
10–19	14.5	80	19.0	101	17.4	104
20–29	27.7	33	28.5	84	18.0	99
30–39	16.2	89	18.1	98	13.9	97
40–49	7.5	102	8.8	94	10.0	95
50–59	4.2	65	5.6	72	10.4	91
60+	5.3	49	5.5	64	15.7	72
Total	100.0	63	100.0	91	100.0	94

[1] Number of males per 100 females.

[2] Figures for 1980, not 1978.

SOURCES: INS, 1978 Statistical Yearbook of the Immigration and Naturalization Service.
Bureau of the Census, 1980 Census of Population, General Population Characteristics, U.S. Summary (PC80-1-B1).

earning and spending units. Their earnings should be determined by numbers of workers, the proportion who work full time, year round, and composition by sex, since women's earnings are only about 60 percent of men's earnings. The 1980 Census shows that median household and family incomes of Koreans in the United States were slightly higher than those of all Americans (see Table 4, Panel A).[8] One reason is that Korean families had more workers than the all-U.S. average (Table 4, Panel C) and, though there are no estimates for households, this was probably true of households too. The number of workers is significant because family income rises in increments of approximately $8 thousand as the number of workers increases from none to one, two, and three or more.

TABLE 4
ECONOMIC AND SOCIAL CHARACTERISTICS IN 1980: U.S. TOTAL AND KOREANS IN THE U.S.

	U.S. Total	Koreans
A. Median Income[1]		
Households	$16,841	$18,145
Families	19,917	20,459
B. Average Family Size	3.27	3.81
C. Average Number of Workers Per Family	1.93	2.09
D. Full-Time, Year-Around Workers As a % Of All Workers		
Male	52.4	50.3
Female	29.0	34.5
E. Share of Women in Employment (Persons Age 16 and Over): %	42.6	52.3
F. Occupation (% Distribution)		
Prof., Tech., Managerial	25.7	28.6
Clerical and Sales	27.3	23.6
Craftsmen and Operatives	26.7	27.2
Laborers and Farmers	7.4	4.0
Service (incl. domestics)	12.9	16.6
Total	100.0	100.0

G.	Education (% Distribution of Schooling Completed, Persons Age 25 And Older)	
	Elementary	18.2	13.6
	High School	49.9	36.9
	College	31.9	49.5
	Total	**100.0**	**100.0**
H.	Regional Distribution (%)	
	Northeast	21.7	19.2
	North Central	26.0	17.5
	South	33.3	19.9
	West	19.0	43.4
	(Pacific)	(14.0)	(39.7)
	Total	**100.0**	**100.0**
I.	Urban-Rural Distribution (%)	
	Urban	73.7	93.0
	Inside Urbanized Areas	61.4	86.9
	Center City	29.6	40.5
	Fringe	31.8	46.4
	Outside Urbanized Areas	12.3	6.1
	Rural	26.3	7.0
	Total	**100.0**	**100.0**

[1] Income figures are for 1979, not 1980.

SOURCES: Bureau of the Census, *1980 Census of Population, U.S. Summaries*, (PC80-1-B1, PC80-1-C1).

Evidence on proportions of fulltime, year–round workers is mixed (see Panel D). Since a higher proportion of Korean than of all–U.S. workers are women and fewer women than men work full time, year–around because of their household and child rearing obligations, when the proportions of fulltime, year–round workers are adjusted by differences in sex composition of the employment totals, one finds that these workers constitute 42 percent of both the Korean and all–U.S. totals. There is therefore no difference in fulltime work or attachment to the labor force, but the higher proportion of women workers would reduce Korean family incomes.

Individual income, or family income divided by the number of family members can be used as a measure of individual welfare. The relatively large size of Korean families (see Panel B) outweighs their higher median incomes so that individual incomes in 1979 were only 88 percent of the all–U.S. level. This reflects lifecycle differences and the higher proportion within the Korean group of young families with children still living at home. Though children's living costs are substantially less than those of adults, the average Korean in America was probably not as well off in 1979 as the average American.[9]

Family incomes should not only vary according to numbers of workers, their labor force attachment and sex composition, but also by occupation and education. The occupational distribution of Korean workers in the United States (Panel F) is very different from that of Korean immigrants with listed occupations (see Table 2) and much more like the all–U.S. than the all–immigrant distribution. One reason is that many of the immigrants in the "housewives, children, and no occupation reported" group have found jobs since arrival in the United States and, unlike those with occupations listed, may hold less desirable service, clerical and sales jobs.[10] A second reason is that migration may be deskilling. Immigrant professionals who have to pass state board examinations for doctors and pharmacists, for example, have to take inferior jobs before the examinations, and possibly afterward as well.[11] This might also explain why the high proportion of professionals among immigrants with listed occupations is not replicated in the occupations of Koreans in the United States. Also, immigrants who are able to maintain their professions may hold the less desirable, lower paying positions, possibly because they are not sufficiently assimilated to have access to the better ones.[12] This last possibility implies that the effect of occupation on income may vary according to immigrants' standing within each occupational income distribution, but I have not found the wage and salary data cross classified by race and occupation that are needed to test this possibility. Information on average income by occupation shows large income gaps between occupations, however, so that even if one does not know where Koreans stand within their occupations, occupational structure should still be an important income determinant. Incomes of service workers, for example, are less than half the incomes of professional, technical, and managerial workers. While incomes of Korean professionals may be at the bottom of the professional income scale, they should still be well above those of service workers.

Education by school level completed of persons age 25 and older in 1980 is presented for all Americans and Koreans in the United States in Panel G of Table 4. Panel G reveals a wide gap at the college level because relatively more Korean immigrants than Americans have completed their college education. Separate distributions for males and females (not shown in the table) are very different for the two groups. They show that Korean females and all U.S. males are educated at the same level, U.S. females are the least educated, while Korean males are most educated (69 percent completed college, a percentage that is about twice as high as those for U.S. males and Korean females). These findings are consistent with evidence of strong educational aspirations among recent Korean male immigrants, who gave "educational opportunity" as their main reason for emigrating to the United States.[13] They are also consistent with a continuing interest in education so that school enrollments among Koreans in America are substantially higher than those of the U.S. population at large in the 22–24 and 25–34 age groups when most people have already completed their education.

Education, whether an investment in skill creation (the human –capital hypothesis) or a means of acquiring credentials (the screening hypothesis), is associated with occupation, particularly in the professional, managerial, and technical categories. One concern here has been the possible downward mobility of immigrant professionals so that Koreans earn below-average incomes in the professional occupations. If this happens, the U.S. income averages by occupation are misleading indicators of Korean emigrants' economic performance. While data needed to assess downward mobility directly are not available, one can compare upper–income shares with college-education shares for the Koreans–in–American and the all–American groups. This comparison makes the usual assumption that education and income are positively related and is designed to see if the effect of education on income is the same for Koreans as for all Americans.

The results of the comparison in 1980, using a family income of $20 thousand as the income cut off, are an earnings/education ratio of 1.04 for Koreans and 1.60 for the United States as a whole. The return to education is evidently lower for Koreans. One possible reason might be that the proportion of female professionals is higher among Koreans in America than in the United States as a whole. However, this is not the case.[14] Another possible reason is that Korean degrees are inferior to American degrees and therefore yield lower incomes. This proposition cannot be tested, but even if Korean degrees were superior so that they represented a greater investment in human capital than their American equivalents, since the quality of Korean education is relatively unknown to American employers, they are likely to regard Korean credentials as inferior to those which are more familiar. This possibility and the handicaps imposed by the assimilation problems of recent immigrants are most likely to reduce the returns to education for Koreans in America.

Regional and urban–rural distributions of Korean and total U.S. populations are presented in the last two panels of Table 4. The regional distribution of Koreans (Panel H) is highly skewed toward the West, particularly the Pacific states, and away from the North Central and Southern regions. The population share of the Northeast is about the same for Koreans and all Americans. That Koreans concentrate in the Pacific states is hardly surprising since most Asian immigrants are concentrated there. Regional distributions of other major Asian groups are even more skewed than the Korean distribution, with over half of the Chinese, two–thirds of Filipinos, and three–quarters of all Japanese living in the Pacific states. Koreans are dispersed by Asian immigrant standards, probably because many of them are orphans and wives of servicemen whose families and husbands do not live in the Pacific states. While Koreans may be less concentrated in the Pacific states than other Asian immigrant groups, they are still much more concentrated than Americans as a whole. This has economic consequences insofar as wages differ by region, possibly because regions vary according to urban–rural makeup. Family incomes in the Pacific states during 1979, for example, were 8 percent more than the U.S. average, while those in the South were 10 percent less. Since Koreans are over–represented in the Pacific states, and under–represented in the South, their regional distribution should serve to raise the incomes of Koreans in America.

The urban–rural distributions of Koreans and the total U.S. population (Panel I) reveal that Koreans are much more urbanized than the population as a whole. Urban concentration, as regional concentration, is typical of most immigrant groups in America and also has implications for income. The median income of rural families in 1979, for instance, was only 87 percent of the median for urban families. While Koreans were more concentrated in center cities than all Americans, and center city incomes were 11 percent below the urban average, this is more than offset by low representation in rural areas. Urban concentration, in consequence, raises the incomes of Korean families.

Urban and regional concentration are two characteristics of Korean immigrants that help to explain why many Koreans have emigrated to America since U.S. immigration restrictions were eased in the late 1960s. The increase in the Korean population of Pacific state cities meant, as time passed, that many more people in Korea had friends and relatives who could help them to settle in America. This network of kin and acquaintances should reduce settling-in costs, and has probably been crucial in many decisions to emigrate. It is obvious why orphans and wives of U.S. servicemen emigrate, but it is not obvious why there are so many of them. The American connections of Korea's network of orphanages, I suspect, are responsible for the major flow of emigrant orphans.[15] The large number of wives results from a major U.S. military presence in Korea, but it would be interesting to know whether a similar presence generates as many emigrant wives in West Germany and the Phillipines.

Increased educational opportunity has undoubtedly been a major cause of emigration from Korea to America, though Korea's educational system is unusually well developed by international standards. Universal primary education was achieved not long after independence and the proportions of secondary and higher-level age cohorts who are enrolled in schools is equivalent to those of countries with much higher per capita incomes.[16] Still, demand for education has been so strong that the Ministry of Education could double the number of openings for college freshmen in 1980 without concern for oversupply. Demand has been strong though families of Korean students pay for two–thirds of the total cost (in school and out of school) of their education, and cost rises with level, especially from high school to college and university.[17] There is an unrequited demand because the Korean educational system, while broad based, is much more restricted at upper levels than is the U.S. system. As recently as the 1970s, only one in four high school students went on to college; the U.S. figure was about one in two.

Another major reason for emigration from Korea to the United States has been greater economic opportunity. The pace of economic development in Korea accelerated in the mid–1960s and, with acceleration, came substantial increases in real family incomes and in individual economic welfare. Incomes were so low before the mid–1960s, however, that in subsequent years there has still been a substantial gap between Korean and U.S. incomes. International income comparisons which use exchange rates to convert local currency denominated incomes to $U.S. are subject to well-known biases but, for what they are worth, the annual income of all urban managerial, professional, technical, and clerical *households* in 1970 was around $1,600. The median wage of professional and technical *workers* in the United States at the time was $11 thousand; that for clerical workers was a little over $7 thousand. When earnings of professional, technical, and managerial households in Korea reached $9,500 in 1979 (clerical workers were excluded from the group by then), the figure for all Korean households in America was around $18 thousand. Even with downward mobility after emigration, Koreans in America were better off than those in Korea. A study by Psacharopoulos of internal rates of return confirms that these earnings differentials influence migration, and that the differential for Koreans in the late 1960s (income after tax, adjusted for cost–of–living differences and differences in the shape of age-earnings profiles) was large enough so that the internal rate of return to Korean professionals who emigrated to the United States was on the order of 400 percent![18]

Other influences on Korean emigration besides the quest for better educational and economic opportunities might include the employment outlook in Korea, Korean government emigration policies, shifts in the political climate, and the state of North –South tensions. Though the pace of development has noticeably quickened since the mid–1960s, the employment outlook cannot have been very bright for most Koreans in recent years. Korea was the prototypical labor–surplus economy in the 1950s and 1960s, and labor was still in surplus until around 1975, when the turning point from surplus to scarcity may have been reached.[19] Before then, opportunities would be better elsewhere, and this was recognized in government sponsored, contract–emigration arrangements under which large numbers of Korean nurses, miners, and construction workers worked in West Germany or for American contractors in Vietnam during the Vietnamese War. These arrangements might have been inspired mainly by the government's need for the foreign exchange generated by remittances from overseas workers, but the government had also been actively promoting a family planning program since the early 1960s to slow the rate of population increase. Except for a law enacted in 1975 to limit emigration by the wealthy, in order to discourage the dollar drain that developed as the wealthy transferred their assets to their new home country, the government has done little to discourage emigration. Emigration has been affected more by U.S. than by Korean policies (over 90 percent of Korean emigrants have emigrated to the United States in recent years) and U.S. policy has responded mainly to national concerns (refugee movements, illegal entry, and domestic labor requirements) rather than to Korea's interest in promoting emigration.

Several recent political events in Korea might have influenced intellectuals and dissidents to emigrate, but it is difficult to assess their impact. One was a constitutional revision in 1972 that ended direct election of the President and the National Assembly, and was a major blow to many Koreans' aspirations for democracy. A second blow came in 1980 when, in the turmoil after President Park's assassination, a military coup ended renewed hope for elections. More significant, perhaps, has been the fear of war that has been aroused by United States withdrawal from Vietnam and incidents on the DMZ (the demilitarized zone or border with North Korea). These events have reminded many Koreans, particularly those who are refugees from the North, of their great vulnerability in case of war in the region. However, political discontent and fear of war have probably been reduced by President Chun's promise to hold elections in 1986, and by renewal of talks between the North and the South since 1984.

Economic Effects of Migration

We know very little about the economic effects of migration, partly because they vary according to viewpoint (global, national, or domestic), partly because they depend on assumptions about the nature of markets and the extent of migration, but mainly because the range of effects is limited only by the analyst's imagination and taxonomic capacities, and we have no way to determine the quantitative significance of many effects. The domestic viewpoint is assumed here since the impact of emigration on Korea is likely to be greater than that of Korean immigration on the United States, and since the policies which affect migration are established by a domestic unit, the nation state.[20] Also, it seems unlikely that the standard neoclassical model applies well to Korean emigration. Many markets are too imperfect to expect that labor and the other factors of production are paid according to their marginal product, and too small to assume constant returns to scale. Since many emigrants are professionals and emigrants as a whole are better educated than those left behind, there are likely to be output losses while replacements are trained.[21] Emigrants are probably wealthier than average and, since they will take as much capital with them as they can, emigration may leave less capital per person for those remaining. Emigration should therefore affect income distribution, alter factor shares, and possibly reduce productivity and incomes of those remaining. In each case, the economic effects of emigration in the sending country are non-neutral. Emigration may still be sufficiently small that such effects are negligible, but this seems unlikely in the Korea of the 1970s and early 1980s.

Two economic aspects of emigration are particularly noteworthy. One is the flow of remittances from emigrants, the other the brain drain, or emigration by scientists, engineers, physicians, and other "high–level" manpower categories. Remittances provide foreign exchange without the usual domestic inputs needed to produce goods and services that must otherwise be exported to earn the foreign exchange; in this sense, remittances are a virtually costless source of foreign exchange.[22] The IMF balance of payments publications list migrants' transfers, workers' remittances, and other private transfers (transfers between individuals or non–official organizations, such as gifts, doweries, inheritances, alimony, and other support payments) under unrequited transfers, but very few countries provide information by separate category. Korea's net unrequited transfers (mainly a credit item) have risen from around $100 million a year in the early 1970s to $500 million a year in the early 1980s, or to approximately 2 to 3 percent of current-account credits. Not all of these are emigrant remittances, but I suspect the figure is still too low to represent actual remittances since a large portion of the total remittance flow is probably arranged through private transactions to avoid foreign-exchange controls, and therefore does not appear in a form where it can be recorded.[23]

There is little direct information on actual remittances, but a survey of migrant professionals based on data from the early 1970s reveals that remittances from Korean students who stayed on to work in the United States averaged around $1,100 dollars a year.[24] Since these are remittances of students and "temporary stay–ons" with low paying jobs or post–doctoral fellowships as well as remittances of "permanent stay–ons," the average for Korean wage earners in the United States should have been considerably higher. Neither student stay-ons nor Koreans in

America as a whole are likely to have been the major source of remittances to Korea, however. The number of overseas contract workers has mushroomed since 1975 with the explosive growth of Korean construction activity in the Middle East. Though reduction of OPEC oil prices has reduced activity, there were still about 170 thousand Koreans working in the Middle East in 1983, and their average remittance was probably well above that of Koreans in America.[25]

Possible benefits from remittances are not only a matter of volume, but also of how remittances are spent. Remittances may be used for consumption or saving, to purchase traded or non-traded goods, imports or domestic output, and may expand the money supply when taken into a country's foreign exchange reserves. This last can be offset by monetary policies that reduce the monetary base, while import licensing arrangements are likely to prevent remittances from adding directly to import demand. More important is the allocation between consumption and saving and between tradables and non–tradables. If remittances go to saving that can be used to finance investment, capacity expansion and income growth will be greater than if remittances are used to finance additional consumption. If the additional demand from remittances goes for tradables, supplies are more likely to increase and results will be less inflationary than if remittances are spent on non–tradables such as land, education, and housing. I have found no information on uses of remittances in Korea, but survey results for Bangladesh may be applicable here. These show that a substantial portion (40 to 45 percent) of remittances goes for consumption, but that families receiving remittances save more than families with the same incomes who receive no remittances, and that the disparity between the two groups rises with income. The survey also shows that most of the savings are used for land purchase, construction and improvement of homes, and debt repayment, and that "the use of these savings for directly productive activities . . . is . . . rather limited."[26]

The brain drain has received widespread attention during the past two decades, not so much as a manpower and development problem, but mainly because acquisition by wealthy nations of scarce human resources from poor nations violates accepted notions of international equity. The issues involved, as with the economic aspects of migration in general, tend to be complex and resistent to practical policy actions. Information available in both Korea and the United States indicates that the problem is significant, particularly from the domestic (i.e., Korean) viewpoint, and

therefore worth examining. The INS publications show that the
United States received about 27 thousand professional and technical immigrants plus another 8 thousand or so students from
Korea who adjusted to permanent resident status during the
1970s. Korean census surveys indicate that employment among
equivalent occupations in Korea rose by 260 thousand from 1970
to 1980. This suggests that over 10 percent of the increment in
Korea's supply of high–level manpower was drained off to the
United States during the decade, and probably more in selected
professions.

A brain drain typically occurs either when professionals
trained in their native country emigrate to other, more economically advanced countries, or when students from less developed
countries stay on after completing their studies in the more
economically advanced countries. All of the human-capital for-
mation occurs in the poor, sending country in the first case, while
some (usually graduate and professional schooling) takes place in
the wealthy, receiving country in the second. The locational
distinction is significant, as is the extent to which education is
publicly subsidized, because both influence the cost of the brain
drain to the sending country.

Costs of public subsidy are presumed to be offset by external
benefits of education, or benefits not captured by the educated in
the form of additional income, but such benefits are lost when the
educated emigrate. Public costs are low in Korea because the
government has shifted most of the educational burden to students' families. External benefits are unknown, but probably no
higher or lower than in other countries, and so we can assume that
net loss (costs less benefits) is probably lower than elsewhere.
Costs—and therefore losses—will also be lower if more students
are educated abroad, while benefits will be greater if more of those
educated abroad return. Actual and stated purposes of emigration
are not necessarily the same, nor do those who emigrate for
"study and training" necessarily leave to obtain professional
(graduate) training. However, the Korean emigration and education statistics can be used to show that in recent years, possibly 20
to 30 percent of Korean professionals have been trained abroad,
mainly in Japan and the United States.[27]

Some of these professionals with foreign training return directly after receiving their degree, others stay for postdoctoral work or
to gain professional experience before returning, while the rest
remain permanently. Brain drain estimates should clearly include
this last group, but what of the intermediate category where the
distinction between staying and leaving is blurred? This compli-

cates estimation, as does the need to rely on statements of intent rather than on actual performance since ex post tests for permanence cannot be wholly complete. It is still possible, however, to ask foreign students whether they plan to stay (temporarily or permanently) after they graduate, and to use their answers to estimate the magnitude of the brain drain. This was done by Tai K. Oh for a sample of Asian students enrolled at major campuses of two "Big Ten" universities in 1968. He found that of the Koreans in the group, 26 percent planned to obtain immigrant visas and remain permanently while 79 percent did not plan to leave the United States immediately after completing their studies.[28] Information on adjustment to permanent resident status from 1971 to 1978 tends to confirm this. About 20 percent of the Korean students who emigrated to the United States during this period did, in fact, apply for permanent residence.[29]

If 20 to 26 percent of Korean students in the United States became permanent residents, then 74 to 80 percent returned to Korea upon graduation or after staying for postdoctoral and professional work. Any loss to Korea from student emigration should therefore be offset by the benefits, both internal and external, derived from education and work in the United States of the students who returned. These benefits are perhaps even more difficult to specify than the costs of the brain drain, but would include the additional income of the returnees associated with their U.S. training plus the external benefits of the added expertise that they have employed in Korea's business, academic, and government circles. Among economists in late 1984, for example, the Minister of Finance, Chief Economic Secretary to the President, and former Deputy Prime Minister obtained their graduate training in the United States. The list could easily be extended to include more economists and leaders in the other sciences and professions.

While some costs and benefits of the brain drain are additive or amenable to economic accounting in concept if not in practice, there are other, qualitative features that have no quantitative counterparts, even conceptual ones. Emigration may be responsible for loss of potential leadership, for example, or loss of national prestige, particularly if those who emigrate are the most aggressive and talented among the country's elite. On the other hand, emigration of good students and professionals may raise national prestige, while ties with emigrant scientists should benefit their sending country. If such qualitative aspects are significant, and quantitative features cannot be weighed in practice, then there is no way to assess the net costs or benefits of the brain drain. This means that some of the recent research on the brain drain is misleading, particularly those studies designed to estimate costs to the sending countries of professionals who emigrate to the United States and other receiving countries. These studies are misleading because the cost estimates are incomplete, in that costs are not reduced by benefits, and because they cannot incorporate qualitative aspects of the brain drain.[30]

Summary and Conclusion

Emigration from Korea to the United States has grown from low levels before U.S. immigration laws were overhauled in 1965 to major proportions in subsequent years. There were 357 thousand Koreans in America in 1980 according to that year's census count, and probably half a million at the end of 1984. Information from this census and INS yearbooks on the demographic, economic, and social characteristics of Koreans in America reveals that more than four of every five are immigrants recently arrived, that they are younger and better educated than the average American, and that there is an unusually high proportion of professionals among those immigrants whose occupations are listed. Koreans, though somewhat more dispersed than other Asian immigrant groups, still live mainly in urban areas and in the Pacific Region as do the other groups. Greater dispersion can be traced to Korean wives of American soldiers who were stationed in Korea and to the unusually large proportion of orphans in the Korean emigrant total.

The easing of U.S. immigration laws may allow more Koreans to emigrate to America, but does not explain why so many have come in recent years. Reasons given earlier include the better educational opportunities and higher incomes that have undoubtedly attracted Koreans to the United States. Also mentioned were the continued North-South tension, worsening of the domestic political climate, and poor employment prospects—particularly before 1975—that should also have made emigration attractive. In addition, as the numbers of emigrants increased, more Koreans in Korea would have friends and relatives in America who could help them to settle and overcome the difficulties that face all new immigrants. Among students, ". . . the most common factor associated with migration . . ." has been ". . . the desire for employment offering opportunities for advancement based on achievement. . . ."[31] Other possible reasons might include the heavy exposure to American culture that has resulted from a large-scale U.S. military presence in Korea, and the unusually rapid growth of the Seoul metropolitan area that has increased anomie and the discontent with the overcrowding and pollution that are typical of over–urbanization.[32] These non–economic reasons have added weight as the conventional economic explanation, which emphasizes the income gap between sending and receiving countries, is inconsistent with recent experience when emigration increased as the U.S.–Korean income gap narrowed.[33]

Migration ought to affect both sending and receiving countries, but only the effects on Korea have been examined here because the economic impact of emigration should be much greater for a small country like Korea than for a large one like the United States. From the Korean or domestic viewpoint, two aspects of interest are remittances and the brain drain. Emigrants and contract workers in the Middle East are major sources of remittances, which rose to $500 million a year from 1981 to 1983. I have found no surveys of how remittances are used in Korea, but if they are spent largely on non–tradables such as land and housing improvements, as elsewhere, they probably have contributed more to speculation in Seoul real estate than to the sort of investment which expands real output.

The brain drain removed more than 10 percent of the increase in Korea's stock of high level manpower between 1970 and 1980 as professionals emigrated to the United States. Emigration by professionals is of particular concern from the domestic viewpoint because they tend to be in short supply in poor countries, they embody heavy investment in human capital, and they cannot always be replaced immediately since training of professionals is a long process. I suspect this concern is not wholly justified, because costs of the brain drain tend to be exaggerated and because foreign training reduces costs. The cost of the brain drain to Korea is not the cost of educating professionals who emigrate, particularly if professional training is received in the United States or elsewhere, nor does cost include the loss of their incomes. Rather, the cost is in the loss of external benefits or in the returns to professional expertise not captured as income by the professionals. This cost is offset to an unknown extent by the benefits of foreign training—both internal and external—of the foreign-trained professionals who return to Korea. These returnees, according to Oh's survey, account for about 74 to 80 percent of the Korean students in the United States, the place where most Koreans go for their advanced training.

Several developments in recent years have probably mitigated or reduced any losses to Korea that might result from the brain drain. One has been the sharp increase in higher education enrollments since the Ministry of Education doubled the number of openings for college freshmen in 1980 in order to eventually double the annual output of college graduates. The other has been the recessions in the United States that have followed oil shocks in 1973 and 1979 to 80. These reduced employment and, when combined with the inability and unwillingness of American universities to adjust the output of graduate students to the new and lower levels of demand, have increased competition for the professional jobs still available. Professional organizations—with the possible exception of the AMA—are usually too weak to restrict competitive imports, unlike the textile, automobile, or steel industries, but they evidently had sufficient political clout in 1976 to persuade Congress to amend the Immigration Act by downgrading the occupational (largely professional) category from third to sixth preference. The effect of this amendment can be seen since 1977 in declining numbers of Koreans admitted to the United States under occupational and other, non-family preferences and in rising numbers admitted under kinship preferences that do not select by education or occupation.

If it is difficult to explain emigration, or to answer the basic questions posed earlier of who migrates, why they migrate, and the economic impact of their migration on sending (and receiving) countries, it is even more difficult to predict what is likely to happen in the future. Nevertheless, something can be said about the likely course of Korean emigration. If the recovery from the 1980 to 1982 recession in the United States can be maintained and the number of job openings continues to expand, emigration should remain at high levels, aided by the large number of Koreans already in America. Though the number of professionals who emigrate is unlikely to reach previous levels in the near future, increasing over–urbanization in Seoul should encourage further emigration of Koreans who qualify under kinship preferences. Many of these are likely to be engaged in business rather than the professions, and will be aided by the presence of Korean trading companies in the United States that supply Korean goods to Korean retailers.[34] Also, these new Korean entrepreneurs are likely to be better financed and therefore to be more formidable competitors than those who emigrated earlier.[35]

I have not dealt with the economic impact of Korean emigration on America so far because there are still too few Koreans in America to have much impact, and because it is as yet too early to assess economic effects. Still, given recent changes in the composition of emigrant flows that have increased the numbers of emigrant entrepreneurs, one can predict that continued large –scale Korean emigration will eventually have an impact on the American business scene. Anyone who has been in mid –Manhattan during the past few years, or in other places where Korean businesses are concentrated, can easily believe that the impact may be substantial.

NOTES

1. A recent review of the literature on the economic causes and consequences of migration is given in Robert E.B. Lucas, "International Migration: Economic Causes, Consequences, and Evaluation," in Mary M. Kritz, et.al., eds. Global Trends in Migration: Theory and Research on International Population Movements (New York: Center for Migration Studies, 1983), pp. 84-109.

2. Continuous residence in the United States for five years is a typical citizenship requirement, so naturalization becomes significant only after six years of residence. Naturalization rates, based on entry six years earlier, ranged from 40 to 67 percent for Koreans in 1966-72, 16 to 30 percent for Japanese, 10 to 27 percent for Chinese, and less than one percent for Mexicans. See Hyung-chan Kim, "Some Aspects of Social Demography of Korean Americans," in Hyung-chan Kim, ed., The Korean Diaspora (Santa Barbara, CA: ABC-Clio, 1977), Table 6.

3. The story of this early Korean emigration is told by Yo-jun Yun, "Early History of Korean Immigration to America," in Hyung-chan Kim, ed., op.cit., pp. 33-46.

4. The 1970 census figure understates the number of Koreans in the United States for several reasons. One is that the census count is based on a sample taken only from states and standard metropolitan areas with Korean populations of more than ten thousand and five thousand, respectively. These cutoffs pose a particular problem in counting Koreans for, unlike Chinese, Japanese, and Filipinos (the other Asian groups tabulated in 1970), Koreans are relatively dispersed and are therefore less likely to live in the West Coast cities where other immigrants from Asia concentrate and are counted. Also, racial and ethnic minorities living in major urban centers (i.e., Koreans) are most likely to be undercounted. In addition, the 1970 tabulation is taken from the number of persons who reported their race as Korean. If birthplace of parents had been used, the count would have been higher. However, where race was not clearly defined or if a person's parents were of different ethnic origins, the father's race (origin) was assigned. Since many Korean women married

non–Asians, the number of Koreans would have been even higher if the mother's race had been used to assign by race.

5.   See Charles D. Keely and Patricia J. Elwell, "International Migration: Canada and the United States," in Mary M. Kritz, et. al., op, cit., pp. 181-207.

6.   Ryu refers to a "Seoul government" statement that the 26,444 South Koreans who immigrated to the United States in 1975 included about 4,600 wives of U.S. servicemen. Since there were 42 thousand U.S. troops in Korea at the time, ". . . one out of every nine . . . who entered Korea for a year of duty exited with a Korean wife." See Jai P. Ryu, "Koreans in America: A Demographic Analysis," in Hyung-chan Kim, ed., op. cit., p. 227.

7.   Also, some of the explanatory variables such as education and occupation are interrelated, which poses a problem of collinearity. The problem is not faced here because I am not attempting to assess the quantitative impact of education, occupation, and the other explanatory variables on income.

8.   Family income includes the incomes of all members age 15 and older who resided with the family at the time of enumeration (April 1980). Household income includes the income of the householder and all other persons age 15 and older who live in the household whether related to the householder or not. Family income is larger than household income because many households consist of the householder only.

9.   The proportion of families with children under 18 living at home in 1980 was 75 percent for Korean families and 52 percent for all–U.S. families. The proportion with children under 6 was 36 and 23 percent, respectively. Conclusions about individual welfare may be misleading because larger families benefit from economies of scale. The BLS surveys of weekly food outlays, for example, show that expenditure per person drops as family size rises.

10.   It is clear that many immigrants who reported no occupation were working in 1980 because there were too few native–born Koreans to account for more than a third of all Koreans employed, while the annual inflow of Koreans with occupations reported during the 1970s was too small to make up more than 40 percent of the remaining employment.

11.   See California Advisory Committee to the U.S. Commission on Civil Rights, Asian Americans and Pacific Peoples: A Case of Mistaken Identity, (Washington, D.C.: U.S.G.P.O., February 1975).

12.   See Illsoo Kim, New Urban Immigrants: The Korean Community in New York, (Princeton, NJ: Princeton University Press, 1981), pp. 156–59.

13.   This finding is reported in a survey by Kim and Condon of recent Korean immigrants living in Chicago and cited in Ryu, op-cit., p. 220

14. In 1980, women made up 24.6 percent of the professional, technical, and managerial group in the United States. The same figure for Korean women in America was 19.9 percent. Since there are relatively more women with a college education among Korean women than among all women in the United States, and since a lower proportion are in professional occupation, a higher proportion are likely to be found in non–professional (i.e., lower paying) jobs, which would lower the earnings/education ratio for Koreans.

15. American connections account for demand, but not for supply. The orphan supply is probably increased by the large–scale U.S. military establishment in Korea, while emigration is promoted by the fact that orphans have no place in Korean society.

16. See Noel F. McGinn, et. al., Education and Development in Korea (Cambridge, Ma.: Harvard University Press, 1980), pp. 61–66. Costs of college and university education in 1970 were more than 40 percent of the family income. Costs in the United States may have been higher or lower, depending in part on opportunity costs in the two countries (i.e.,—earnings foregone to attend school), but what is probably more important was the rapid rise of costs in Korea. See Illsoo Kim, op. cit., p. 79.

17. Noel F. McGinn, et. al., op. cit., pp. 15–29.

18. George Psacharopoulos, "Estimating Some Key Parameters in the Brain–Drain Taxation Model," in J.N. Bhagwati, ed., The Brain Drain and Taxation (Amsterdam: North-Holland Press, 1976), Vol. II, pp. 53–62.

19. See Bai Moo-ki, "The Turning Point in the Korean Economy," The Developing Economies, Vol. 20. No. 2 (June 1982), pp. 117–40.

20. The Korean government may be concerned with the economic welfare of all Koreans (national viewpoint), but its economic policies apply mainly to those in Korea rather than to Koreans living elsewhere. Emigration should affect Korea more than immigration the United States because Korea's population is smaller (in 1970, there were 6.5 Americans for every Korean).

21. Of the quarter of a million or so Korean emigrants to the United States in 1970–1980, approximately 33–34 thousand were professionals. Almost half of the Koreans in America in 1980 had completed college when the figure for Koreans in Korea was 8 percent.

22. This is not strictly true if the emigrant's sending country loses external benefits that might accure in the emigrant's presence.

23. Foreign–exchange controls limit dollar purchases of Koreans travelling abroad, transfers to students studying abroad, etc. Such controls encourage dollar transactions between Koreans needing more dollars in the United States and those already in the United States with dollars to send to Korea, and discourage transactions in which remit-

tances would otherwise be converted from dollars to *won* by Korean banks.

24.   See William A. Glaser, *The Brain Drain: Emigration and Return*, United Nations Institute for Training and Research, Report Number 22 (London: Pergamon, 1975), pp. 210-11.

25.   Unlike most Koreans in America, Korean workers in the Middle East are wage earners rather than dependents and must send remittances to support their immediate families. Worker remittances are also likely to be high because consumption is restricted in the Middle Eastern construction camps.

26.   Syed Ashraf Ali, *et. al.*, *Labor Migration from Bangladesh to the Middle East*, World Bank Staff Working Paper No. 454 (Washington, D.C.: World Bank, April 1981), p. 136. See also Tables 3.17 and 3.18. Others have also noted that ". . . a considerable portion of remittance induced expenditures are on nontraded goods such as land, housing, and education." See Charles W. Stahl, "Labor Emigration and Economic Development", *International Migration Review*, Vol. 16, No. 4 (Winter 1982), p. 874.

27.   This estimate relates numbers of emigrants who leave for "study and training" *each year* to Korean graduate school enrollments in 1976-81 and assumes that graduate training takes three years on an average.

28.   Tai K. Oh, *The Asian Brain Drain: A Factual and Causal Analysis* (San Francisco: R & E Research Associates, Inc., 1977), pp. 32-33.

29.   This calculation should be adjusted for lag between entry and application for adjustment, and also for the fact that a few students hold immigrant visas on arrival, but such refinement is unlikely to alter the finding significantly.

30.   A case in point is the estimate of $56 million as the educational cost to Korea of immigrant scientists, engineers, physicians and surgeons entering the United States in fiscal years 1971 and 1972. See Congressional Research Service, *Brain Drain: A study of the Persistent Issue of International Scientific Mobility*, a study prepared for the Subcommittee on National Security Policy and Scientific Development of the Committee on Foreign Affairs, U.S. House of Representatives (Washington, D.C.: U.S. Government Printing Office, September 1974), Table 25, p. 156. Also, the appropriate cost to Korea is not educational cost as measured in this study, which is a sunk cost, but society's return on education, or any social product in excess of the educated individual's consumption. See Charles W. Stahl, *op. cit.*, p. 881.

31.   Tai K. Oh, *op. cit.*, p. 72.

32.   See Ilsoo Kim, "Korean Emigration Connections to Urban Amer-

ica: A Structural Analysis of Premigration Factors in South Korea."
(Paper presented before the Conference on Asia–Pacific Immigration to
the United States, sponsored by the East–West Population Institute,
Honolulu, Hawaii, September 20-25, 1984), pp. 9-10, 13-14.

33.   There is evidence that higher per capita income and higher
average growth rates are negatively associated with return of emigrant
students. See William Glaser, *op. cit.,* pp. 29-32. One possible reason is
that the macroeconomic averages can cancel increasing income inequality so that ". . . employment, prosperity, and morale of professionals may
lag even when GNP is growing for the economy as a whole," (*Ibid.,* p. 33).
This may have happened in Korea if the inflation associated with rapid
development reduced the relative income of salaried professionals whose
salaries often lag behind inflation, but such a decline has not been
substantiated. There is evidence, however, that income inequality increased after 1965 in Korea, and part of this increase may have been due
to a lag in professional incomes. See Government of the Republic of
Korea, *The Fifth Five Year Economic and Social Development Plan,
1982-1986,* English Version (Seoul, 1982), p. 9.

34.   Ilsoo Kim, "Korean Emigration Connections . . . ," p. 16

35.   In early 1984, the Korean government raised the amount of
foreign currency that business emigrants to Canada were allowed to take
with them. Having done this, the government may well do the same for
business emigrants to the United States. See Jung Keun Kim, "The Trends
and Policies of Korean Emigration." (Paper presented before the Conference on Asia–Pacific Immigration to the United States, sponsored by the
East–West Population Institute, Honolulu, Hawaii, September 20-25,
1984), p. 5.

CHAPTER 3

INDIAN EMIGRATION: ITS DIMENSION AND IMPACT ON INDIAN ECONOMY

M.C. Madhavan

Introduction

International labor migration and associated movements in recent decades have assumed significant proportions, almost equal to those of the trans–oceanic exodus of Europeans during 1840 to 1930.[1] The U.S. admitted 10.8 million immigrants from 1950 to 1981, and Canada about 2.5 million.[2] Bohning (1984b:381) estimates that western European countries now host 6.5 million migrant workers plus at least as many dependents. The Middle Eastern countries had three million migrant workers plus one million dependents in 1980. Migrants in South America may be estimated at about 3.5 to 4 million, in West Africa 1.3 million, and in South Africa 0.3 million. Of those who entered Australia with the intention of settling there permanently , about 2.1 million might have stayed there as of 1980. New Zealand had over 0.4 million foreign born population in 1971 and 42,000 settlers arrived in 1980. Nearly 4 million Indians are estimated to have migrated to nearby countries (Nepal, Sri Lanka, Malaysia and Singapore) during the last 30 years.

Between 10.3 and 14.5 million undocumented migrants live in different parts of the world. To this must be added legally admitted non-immigrant workers in the U.S., and foreign workers and their dependents in Australia, Canada and New Zealand. Some of those admitted as permanent immigrants have returned to the countries of their origin.[3] Thus the number of people living in countries outside their country of birth, either as settlement immigrants (and naturalized citizens of the receiving country), contract immigrants or as undocumented migrants may be around 50-55 million in 1981.[4] Of this, approximately 60 percent might have originated in developing countries (United Nations, Dept. of International Economic and Social Affairs, 1982:69), one–sixth of which is likely to be from India (see Table 1).

International migration affects economic activities in both migrant–sending and migrant–receiving countries. The short–run effects of migration may vary from their long–run impact on economic growth. Studies concerned with the economic and social effects of international migration have been limited largely to the industrialized countries,[5] and only recently have there been attempts to deal with effects of emigration from developing countries' point of view.[6] In his important work Friendlander (1965) analyzed the impact of emigration from Puerto Rico on its economy and concluded that it was a crucial variable in the economic growth and prosperity of Puerto Rico. Yet he was careful not to generalize about the usefulness of emigration for all developing countries desiring rapid economic growth.

A comprehensive study of labor migration from Bangladesh to the Middle East was undertaken recently by Ali, et al. for the World Bank (1981). It concluded that "The net present value from migration is not only positive but also quite large. . . . We have not, however, taken into account certain cost elements such as the psychological costs of separation from the family or the disloca-tion costs arising from a mass re–entry of migrants. But the statistical magnitude of such cost components would have to be very large to reverse our findings of sizeable net social gain from emigration." Such optimism of the beneficial effect of emigration on a developing country is not shared by Fergany (1982), who, after reviewing the emigration from Yemen Arab Republic to the Middle East, suggests that emigration would be detrimental to the economic development of Yemen Arab Republic. Some aspects of economic and social consequences of Indian emigration to the Middle East have been studied by Nair (1983), Gulati (1983), and Weiner (1982), focusing on the state of Kerala, which accounts for the largest proportion of Indian emigrants in the Middle East. No in–depth study of Indian emigrants throughout the world seems to exist. An attempt is made in this paper to fill this gap.

Dimensions of Indian Emigration

This study is concerned with people born in India who have become either permanently settled in another country or have contractual obligations to work for at least one year.[7] Indian students in host countries, official and business migrants, and visitors, even if they stay for more than one year, are not treated here as residents of those countries in which they live. Statistical and conceptual problems involved in measuring long–term migration are immense[8] and data drawn from many sources are not strictly comparable. Insofar as it was necessary and feasible, adjustments were made to correspond to the above definition, but no attempt was made to arbitrarily estimate the number of Indian immigrants or people of Indian origin in areas where they are included along with Pakistanis, Sri Lankans, and other Asian groups.

Emigration Prior to the Second World War

Indian emigration in modern times dates back to the last decade of the 18th century, when a small number of Indians migrated on their own to nearby countries such as Ceylon (now Sri Lanka), Malaya and Burma in search of opportunities to acquire wealth.[9] But the major thrust of Indian emigration came after the abolition of slavery in the British territories from 1833 to 34. To fill the gap in the supply of labor created by the emancipation of slaves, colonial planters and government turned to India (Sandhu 1969:76). This system of labor importation came to be known as indentured emigration. In return for passage and a wage, the emigrant undertook to work for a specified employer for a period of three to five years. The employers made the laborers work as hard and as long as possible under inhospitable conditions.[10] Justice J. Beaumont, a former chief justice of British Guiana (now Guyana) described the indenture as "a monstrous, rotten system, rooted upon slavery, grown in its stale soil, emulating its worst abuses, and only the more dangerous because it presented itself under false colours, whereas slavery (had) the brand of infamy written upon its forehead" (quoted in Sandhu). It created such opposition in the British Isles that the British government finally abolished the indenture system around 1916.

The indenture labor emigration from India was the major source of labor supply for sugar plantations in Fiji, the West Indies and Mauritius, and for the construction of the Uganda Railway,[11] but it was insufficient to meet the needs of plantation owners in Ceylon and Malaya. To meet such requirements, a new system of recruiting free labor in India, known as the *Kangani* system, came into existence, first in Ceylon and later extended to Malaya.[12] It vastly improved the labor supply to Malaya and Ceylon, but its method of recruitment left much to be desired. It came under severe attack for gross violations of law. Though laborers were supposed to be free, in practice they were not mobile, mainly because of cash advances that tied them into a cycle of debt bondage.[13] The system was finally abolished in 1938, when the Indian government placed a ban on assisted labor migration.

In the waning days of the *Kangani* system of labor recruitment, independent labor migration, both assisted and non–assisted, emerged as important migrant streams and became significant after the depression, when Indian laborers migrated to Burma, Malaya, Ceylon and East Africa to work in unskilled and semi-skilled occupations. The long and hard work of Indian labor migrants helped enrich the planters, labor recruiters and money lenders, but there was no discernible improvement in the economic conditions of most migrant laborers. Omvedt (1980:189) recently observed that they "toiled in disease ridden conditions to provide sugar, coffee, tea and other raw materials for the industries of Europe, and built up the major export industries in several countries—they also ended up having only a precarious basis as a low status and distrusted minority in the societies they entered, and sometimes with no citizenship at all."

In contrast to the miserable condition of Indian labor migrants in the British Colonies, non–labor migrants fared much better, and some groups even prospered.[14] The earliest commercial migrants such as merchants, financiers and construction contractors can be traced back to the late 18th century. Over the years, they did so well that they became important economic actors.[15] Indians also proved to be invaluable in the clerical and technical services of colonial governments, and Indian Sikhs were sought after for duties such as policemen, caretakers and guards. These people received better salaries and wages than what they would have earned in British India.[16] Besides, there was a continuous flow of commercial immigrants in the 20th century from India to Ceylon, Malaya, Burma, Kenya, Uganda, Tanganika, Zanzibar, Persian Gulf States, Hong Kong and Fiji. The vast majority of them were salesmen, petty entrepreneurs, traders, shopkeepers and streetside vendors. Commercial migrants to the British Colonies would have been about one–fifth of the total Indian migrants up to the beginning of World War II.

Estimates of Indian emigrants made on the basis of data available to the author suggest that about 3.1 million (see Table 2) Indians might have migrated to different parts of the world up to 1945.[17] Of this, 2.2 million went to Ceylon, Burma and Malaysia; 420,000 to East Africa and Mauritius; 400,000 to the West Indies and Fiji; and 50,000 to the United States, United Kingdom, Canada and other countries. Nearly four–fifths of the Indian emigrants were agricultural laborers who had little or no education, had endured uncertain and difficult economic conditions at home and had hoped that emigration would help them and their families to get out of the curse of poverty. Many of these people returned to India when they experienced far worse conditions in the foreign countries than the one they left behind, but most of them settled down permanently in the country of their immigration after fulfilling the contractual obligation to the planters. Among non–labor migrants, many returned occasionally to India, taking with them part of their earnings for investment in India, mainly in houses and jeweleries. Most of the merchants and financiers returned to India periodically and used part of their accumulated wealth for traditional investment in homes and for initiating new enterprises in India.[18]

Emigration Pattern Since the War

Important changes have ocurred in Indian international migration patterns since 1945. Nepal, a neighboring country with close socio–cultural ties with India, has become the most important place of destination for Indian emigrants. The number of people of Indian origin living in Nepal was estimated at 3.2 million in April 1981 by the Indian Minister of External Affairs.[19] After allowing for natural growth in population, this would imply an inflow of about 2.8 million since 1961, when the Nepalese census report classified 76,311 Indians as "foreign citizens." Our estimates suggest another 1.2 to 1.7 million Indian emigrants would have migrated to different parts of the world in the last 35 years (see Table 2).

Nearly 750,000 Indian emigrants have become permanent residents in developed countries, with the United Kingdom accounting for 40 percent of that inflow, the United States for 28 percent, Canada for 14 percent, Western Europe (excluding the U.K.) for 11 percent, and Australia for 5 percent. Indian emigration to the United Kingdom was constrained after the passage of the Commonwealth Immigrants Acts of 1962 and 1971, yet over 200,000 Indians migrated to the U.K. during the 1960's, mainly because the law permitted the flow of professionals and skilled people and their dependents, and the dependents of the pre–1962 residents.[20] There was a reduced flow of Indian immigrants into the U.K. in the 1970s, but it seems to have made a small recovery in 1978 and 1979.[21] Large inflows into the U.S., Canada, western Europe and Australia are mainly due to changes in their immigration policies to emphasize skills rather than national origin as the major determinant of immigration into those countries. Indian immigrants as a proportion of all immigrants admitted into the U.S. have risen from 1 percent during 1965–1969 to 4 percent in 1975–1979.

About 950,000 people born in India live in the Middle Eastern countries, most of whom migrated during the 1970's. They comprise contract immigrants and their dependents and they are aware that they have to return to India. Malaysia, Singapore, and East African countries have become progressively less important as major destinations due, in part, to restrictive immigration policies in force in these countries. Only the professionals who are on contract for service, and their dependents, wives and children of citizens, and individuals who can bring in considerable amounts of wealth for investment are admitted as immigrants into Malaysia and Singapore. Earlier Indian immigrants to Sri Lanka, Burma, Kenya, Uganda and Tanzania have left those countries in record numbers either to return to India or to go to other destinations such as the U.S., Canada and Western Europe. There has been migration of India–born professionals and commercial people to Hong Kong, Nigeria, Ethiopia, Zambia, Sudan, Aden, Brazil, New Zealand, Iran and others, not exceeding 70,000.

After careful review of available evidence, it is estimated that in 1981 there were 5.0 to 5.5 million persons (2.2 to 2.7 million excluding Nepal) born in India living in different parts of the world (see Table 1), amounting to 0.73 to 0.81 percent of the population of India in 1981. The Indian government perceives emigration to be not demographically significant, and the present situation is satisfactory (United Nations 1982:189). The population of Indian origin living outside India may be between 13.2 to 13.8 million[22] (10.0 to 10.6 million, excluding Nepal). Compared to Wilcox's estimate (1929:142) of 2.1 million Indians domiciled abroad as of 1924, they have almost quintupled in the last 57 years (increased over 550 percent, including the migration to Nepal).

Characteristics of Emigrants

Information on occupational, educational, age and socio-cultural characteristics of Indian emigrants are few and far between. Beyond recent attempts to collect such information for emigrants to the Middle East from the state of Kerala (Nair 1983) through village and regional surveys, no organized machinery seems to exist in India to gather data in a comprehensive manner. Some information about Indian immigrants in the United Kingdom have been collected through sample surveys (Aurora 1967, Davision 1966, Desai 1963, Rex and Tomlinson 1979, Rose 1969). Many of the immigration and naturalization departments of the immigrant-receiving countries collect information on occupational, age and sex characteristics of Indian immigrants. The U.S. Immigration and Naturalization Service publishes such data annually (see Tables 3 and 4). The U.S. averages have been used in this study to estimate the occupational distribution of Indian immigrants in Australia and western Europe (excluding the U.K.). Canadian Immigration Department data on occupational distribution of Indian immigrants' intentions are extensive but incomplete, because a large number of them have not expressed the nature of the occupation they will pursue. Hence, Indian immigrants' occupational characteristics are estimated upon the assumption that the proportion of Indian immigrants in the professional, technical and kindred workers category will be more than the average for all immigrants in the same category during the period 1969 to 1975, and the proportion of Indian immigrants in sales, clerical, craft and operative categories will be less. Proportions of Indian immigrants in various occupations in the United Kingdom are based on information in Rose (1969:85, 86, 176 and 183), Hill (1970:32-33), and the Central Statistical Organization (1982:26) about the occupational status of heads of households, arrivals of voucher holders and dependents and net immigration.

Indian immigrants' occupational characteristics in the Middle East are based on survey results reported in Nair (1983) and interviews with a business leader in the construction business in the Middle East.[23] Indian labor force characteristics reported in Swee-Hock (1970:130) and in Sandhu (1969) formed the basis to determine the occupational characteristics of Indian immigrants in Singapore and Malaysia. Hong Kong distribution is based on information obtained from a person who is a part of the Indian business community in Hong Kong. No source was available to the author to determine the occupational distribution of Indian immigrants in Nepal, most of whom might be in the last two categories of occupational classification referred to in Table 5.

Estimates of occupational distribution of Indian immigrants in most important receiving countries, given in Tables 5 and 6, should be taken more as indicative than definitive of the type of Indians emigrating to other countries. Unlike in the pre–World War II period dominated by poorly educated agricultural labor emigrants mainly to the British Colonies, there has taken place a significant change in the composition of Indian emigrants. India-born members in the labor force of other countries (excluding Nepal) would be around 1.2 million. Two out of nine in the labor force are well qualified professionals, such as doctors, dentists, engineers, scientists, professors, administrators, managers and other professional people. Four in nine comprise skilled technicians, sales and clerical personnel, and the rest are farm workers, and unskilled and semi-skilled workers. Nearly 70 percent of Indian emigrants have gone to developing countries and 30 percent have settled down in developed countries (Table 6).

What is significant is that the pattern of Indian emigration to developed countries is strikingly different from that of developing countries. The major reasons for this type of migrant flow are the sustained high demand for trained personnel in the 1970s in the developed countries, the greater international mobility of professional categories and the greater selectivity introduced into the admittance criteria of several industrialized immigrant receiving countries.[24] Relatively less qualified persons in the third and fourth categories of occupational classification account for over 90 percent of Indian immigrant flow into developing countries, as against only 50 percent for developed countries. Conversely, highly qualified professional people constitute 50 percent of the total flow to developed countries, and only 10 percent in developing countries. Developed countries attracted over two–thirds of professionally qualified Indian emigrants, about one–fourth of sales, clerical and skilled persons and about one–sixth of others. While the United Kingdom received over 85 percent of unskilled and semi–skilled Indian immigrant labor that migrated to developed countries and 70 percent of skilled, clerical and sales persons, the United States accounted for about one–half of immigrant professionals admitted into developed countries. The Middle Eastern countries provided opportunities for two–thirds of all India–born unskilled and semi–skilled workers and four–fifths of skilled, clerical and sales persons who migrated to developing countries.

Occupational composition of Indian immigrant labor force in the U.S. was much more professionally and technically oriented than the labor force in the nation as a whole. Over 80 percent of the Indian immigrant labor force in 1981 was engaged in professional, technical and management categories of employment (Table 4) against 27 percent for the nation (U.S. Department of Commerce 1984). One in seven professionally or technically qualified persons who migrated to the U.S. during 1965 to 1979 was an Indian.[25] Such differences between the quality of the Indian immigrant labor force and that of Canada and Australia are also discernible, but may not be to the extent of those in the U.S. In the United Kingdom, however, the proportion of Indian immigrants engaged in professional fields in 1981 was somewhat lower than the corresponding national rate. The composition of Indian migrant occupation in most of the developing countries seems to be heavily weighted in the direction of skilled, clerical, sales, unskilled and semi–skilled categories.

Data on age characteristics of Indian immigrants are limited to only a few developed countries, and recent surveys in Kerala shed some light on Indians going to the Middle East. Generally, one would expect migrants to be over represented in the young working age group and children and the aged would be expected to be under represented, compared to the total population (United Nations, Department of Economic and Social Affairs 1979:54). Indian migrant movements follow this general pattern, but what is interesting is that they are far more concentrated in the working age group than the ratio for migrants from all other countries. Almost 75 percent of the Indian immigrants to the U.S. during 1964 to 1981 were in the age group of 20 to 49, as compared to 68 percent for all immigrants.[26] In recent years, this proportion is declining for Indians, going from 81.6 percent in 1971 to 66.2 percent in 1981, which is still much higher than the ratio of 55.2 for all immigrants. In Canada, 62.5 percent of immigrant Indians during 1980 to 1981 were in the 20 to 59 age group, compared to 59 percent for all immigrants.[27]. The Indian immigrant population in the U.K. in the 15 to 44 age group are estimated to be around 57 percent of the total Indian population, slightly over the ratio for all immigrants. Village surveys taken in Kerala reveal that over 80 percent of Indians going to the Middle East are less than 35 years old, and almost all of them are under 50.

Sex structure changes also followed the general pattern observed in different stages of migration. In the early stage when migrants respond to a high labor demand, they are likely to be predominantly males. Once the migrants feel secure in their jobs, their dependents join them, reducing the male–female ratio. In the early years of Indian emigration to the U.S., the male–female ratio was 1.5 during 1965 to 1969. This declined to 1.08 during 1975 to 1979, with the average for the period 1965 to 1979 being 1.16. This ratio in the U.K. was 1.18 during 1950 to 1971, varying between 1.8 in the early 1950s and 0.92 in the late 1960s and early 1970s. In Canada, female Indian immigrants outnumbered male immigrants in recent years, compared with the ratio of 1.41 in the early 1970s. Indian migration to Australia was well balanced such that sex ratio was 1.07 during 1960 to 1973. The declining trend in this ratio in Western countries may, in part, be attributed to the family unification provisions of their immigration policies. In contrast to the declining ratio in the above countries where Indian immigrants have settled down permanently, the ratio is rather high in countries such as Kuwait and Saudi Arabia, where most Indian immigrants have gone on fixed term contracts.

Though emigrants came from every corner of India, some regions played a larger role than others. In the pre–war period, the southern Indian states were more important than others in the emigration to Burma, Ceylon, Malaya and Mauritius (Sandhu 1969), Bengal and the Central Provinces to the West Indies (Nath 1970), Gujarat to south and east Africa, and Punjab to the U.S., Canada and Hong Kong (Rose 1969). Detailed data about emigration are not available for the post-World War II period. Fragmentary data suggest that emigration to the Middle East mainly originate in Kerala, Andhra Prdesh, Punjab, Gujarat, Goa, Maharastra and Tamildadu (Nair 1984), to Nepal in Bihar, Assam and Uttar Pradesh, and to the U.K. in Punjab and Gujarat. All the states mentioned above have contributed to emigration to the U.S., Canada, Australia and West European countries excluding the U.K..

Kerala, which has the highest unemployment rate in India (Table 7) is one of the leading states in the supply of emigrants. Nair reports that as many as 1.8 million Keralites may live outside India. Goa, Tamilnadu and Andhra Pradesh, with high unemployment rates, have also contributed a large number of emigrants. However, what is surprising is that both Punjab and Gujarat, with relatively low unemployment rates, have also been major actors in the emigration process. Both these groups have been great wanderers in the last 100 years within and outside India. The partition of the Indian Subcontinent displaced many Punjabis and, to some extent, dispossessed them. This might have been a contributing factor in Punjabis seeking their fortune in other countries. The business acumen of Gujaratis is rather well known and they have tried to use every opportunity open to them within and outside India.

Causes of Emigration

In general, the decision to emigrate is made in three steps. First, the prospective emigrant collects information about the employment possibilities for people with his or her skills in the prospective countries of immigration, and transportation costs, living costs, potential salary, legal restrictions, and such other data that will facilitate his decision making process. Second, he or she attempts to assess direct monetary benefits and costs, indirect non-monetary benefits and costs to him- or herself and family members, and then he or she decides whether direct and indirect benefits exceed relevant costs. If they do, he or she will want to emigrate to another country. Third, to actualize the desire, either the prospective immigrant uses his or her family's financial resources or will attempt to obtain financial support from an institution or individual in the prospective country of immigration. In cases where the emigrant has problems in obtaining accurate information on some of the variables mentioned above, he or she is guided by the experience of people in his or her area

who have been to, or still live in, the prospective area of immigration.

No attempt has been made in India to model the emigration
decision making process, due in part to the difficulties associated
with measuring some of the variables. Yet surveys to date partially
capture the quintessence of the emigration process. Wage differentials that exist between India and a foreign country seem to have
been the greatest pull toward emigration. Nair (1983) has gathered
information from returning Indians which suggest very large wage
differentials between India and Persian Gulf countries. Wage
differentials between western countries and India are rather well
known. In the case of highly specialized fields, many opted to stay
in the country where they received their graduate training, mainly
because there was no scope in India in the past for those
disciplines. Many scientists and medical doctors who returned to
India to work wanted to emigrate to avoid isolation—loss of
contact with colleagues through inability to travel, to receive
visitors, and to have access to journals and specialized reviews
(UNESCO 1984:428). The growing conflict in different regions in
India between "sons of the soil" and the "outsiders" (Weiner
1978:3), a slow rate of progress up the professional ladder,
oversupply of trained people in one's field, the desire to be
independent and to avoid potential conflict between one's wife
and mother are some of the contributing factors for emigration
from India.

Impact On Indian Economy

The impact of emigration on economic growth will depend on the
size of emigration in relation to population growth, characteristics
of emigrants, the amount of emigrants' remittances and its dispo-
sition, and the extent of association and involvement in development projects emigrants have with the country of birth.[28]

Emigration and Population Growth

Emigration can help to control and reduce population growth of a
country in the short and long run. Since it will withdraw
reproductive population, it could help reduce the birth rate in the
future. The impact of emigration on the population growth of
India and birth rate was minimal, since the size of emigration

from India in any one recent decade was only around 2 percent of decennial population growth.[29] In states such as Kerala, Andhra Pradesh, Tamilnadu, Goa, Gujarat and Punjab which seem to have accounted for substantial outflow of Indians to foreign countries, population growth rates during 1970s were the lowest with the exception of Gujarat, and birth rate declines were generally higher than other states in India. However, the significance of emigration in the reduction of population growth and birth rate cannot be determined without further analysis of the contribution of other factors to the reduction, including birth control education and internal migration.

Emigration, Unemployment and Productivity

Productivity growth in the economy will also be affected by emigration, and it will depend on whether the emigrant was unemployed or employed at the time of migration; skilled or unskilled; replaceable or not from the labor available within the country at no additional cost; wage paid to the emigrant was equal to, less than or higher than the migrant's marginal revenue product; international competitive position of the industry in which the emigrant was employed is eroded or not; and whether emigration raises the ratios of land to labor and capital to labor. There are many combinations of the above conditions, and it is impossible to determine the effect of each combination on productivity growth. The positive effect in the short run on productivity growth is posited on the assumption that emigrants are mainly either from the unemployed, unskilled and redundant labor force or from the skilled pool replaceable at no extra cost.

Ideally, disaggregated data by industry and skill level classification would be necessary to determine the effect of emigration on industrial productivity changes. Such data are not available for India. Hence the flows of emigration by broad occupational classifications are analyzed to determine whether such outflow would have created shortages in the economy and consequently would have had adverse effects on the economy. The total number of India–born professional, technical and kindred workers who migrated to different parts of the world up to 1981 was approximately 232,800 (see Table 6), which is about 28 percent of those unemployed in 1981. This outflow seemed to have reduced the pressure of educated unemployment.

Existence of such a level of unemployment among technically

qualified people in India is the result of faulty manpower planning.[30] Whereas, in industrial countries, 70 percent of students trained in science go into industries, in developing countries, such as India, only 10 percent go into industry, resulting in heavy pressure on the universities and research institutes to employ students trained in science[31] (for the extent of unemployment among technically and scientifically trained people, see Table 8). Since the ability of the institutions of higher learning to absorb the stock of unemployed people in these categories, (about 340,000 persons in 1981, including 86,000 engineering diploma holders, and annual flow of about 90,000)[32] are limited, there is a "skill drain" from India. However wasteful "skill drain" may be from the point of view of a developing country, some contend that it is not as bad as the problem of "skill waste" or "brain waste," a condition of maladjustment of human resource within a country as reflected in the concentration of professional and technical people in urban centers.[33]

"Skill drain" is very expensive from the point of view of India. Its opportunity cost may be low or even near zero, in the short run, for certain categories. However, the long run cost to society is likely to be very high since the professional and technical emigrants constitute the elite human resource which is essential for development (UNESCO 1984 and Whelan 1974).

There were about 22,000 managers and administrators among the emigrants from India (Table 6). Almost no growth in unemployment in this category during 1974 to 1981 suggests that emigration might have siphoned off most of those who were trained in India during this period. Since high caliber management specialists are in high demand, their departure to greener pastures will imply a high social cost to India, and productivity growth in industries with inefficient management would certainly have been adversely affected.[34]

Nearly 420,000 laborers, service workers and farm laborers, a tiny portion of the millions of unemployed or underemployed people in this category, have migrated to other countries. The positive effect this would have had on productivity is so miniscule that it did not matter very much in improving the living conditions of all those who were left behind, excepting the family members, close relatives and friends of the emigrants.

Salespersons, clerks, craftsmen and operatives numbering over 487,000 emigrated during this period. They accounted for over 20 percent of those who still remain unemployed in India (Table 6). While the departure of salespersons and clerks did not seem to have created any shortages, the emigration of well trained persons in nursing, electronics, machine building and maintenance, metallurgy, construction and other fields would have had a far more damaging effect on growth in productivity than even the emigration of professionals (UNESCO 1984). Therefore, it is uncertain what would have been the net effect on productivity of migration of skilled workers, salespersons and clerks.

The foregoing discussion of the effect of emigration from India on productivity growth suggests that emigration has certainly helped to ease the pressure of unemployment considerably in certain categories, but the evidence of the impact of emigration on Indian productivity is inconclusive.

Emigrant's Remittances and Balance of Payments

On the other hand, emigrants' remittances and deposits in non–resident accounts in Indian Commercial Banks have played a significant role in improving India's balance of payments position. Private unrequited transfers have risen so sharply in the 1980s that they are equal to about 30 percent of India's exports (Table 10). Whether they continue to be as important as they have been in recent years will depend on the size of the Indian emigrant population, their earnings level, perception of their jobs as permanent or temporary and of the host country's attitude toward new immigrants, visa status, the number of dependents an emigrant has in the country of settlement and in India, knowledge about investment opportunities in India and around the world, length of stay in host country and other factors. Such data are not available; nor do we have detailed information on the sources of inflows by country or occupational classification. It is impossible, therefore, to undertake any analysis of determinants of emigrants' remittances to project into the future. Hence, discussion will be limited to examining the influence of emigrants' remittances and non-resident account bank deposits on India's balance of payments, savings and investments, and wage and price levels in some areas where emigration is significant.

Private unrequited transfers estimates given by the International Monetary Fund exclude credits in lieu of contra-entries for imports from the U.S. under Public Law 480 (Titles II and III), but presumably include certain unilateral transfers such as receipts of missionaries in India from foreign countries which are not distinguished by the Reserve Bank of India in the data they collect.

Since non–emigrant related private flows are not likely to be significant and would not have changed their share in the total substantially enough to affect the rates of growth in emigrants' remittances, private unrequited transfers data are used in place of emigrants' remittances.

These transfers, after following a zigzag pattern during 1960 to 1973, increased tenfold during 1973 to 1979 and almost doubled again in 1980[35] when the total amounted to $2,743 million. After declining in 1981, it seemed to have recovered in 1982 as evidenced in the nine months estimate of $1,878 million.[36] Much of the increase in emigrants' remittances since 1970 is from sterling area countries (excluding Canada), its share in the total increasing from 53.4 percent in the early 1970s to 59.9 percent in the 1980s (Table 10). Yet it should be noted that remittances from non-sterling area countries increased almost 150 percent between the late 1970s and early 1980s.[37]

The balance of payments current account is strengthened very much by inflows of remittances which helped to finance an increasing part of the merchandise trade deficit from 11.2 percent in the early 1960s to 46.6 percent[38] in the early 1980s, and of the balance on goods and services from 8.1 percent to 46.5 percent (Table 10). They also have become more important as a major source of foreign exchange earnings to meet developmental needs. As a proportion of merchandise exports, it has increased from over 5 percent in the early 1960s to 30 percent in the early 1980's, and as a proportion of service exports, from 38 percent to 65 percent. Emigrants' transfers have grown to such an extent that its total of $5,024 million during 1980 and 1981 exceeded the total foreign assistance utilized by about $100 million.[39]

Besides, the capital account side of the balance of payments is also fortified by the inflow of deposits in non–resident accounts maintained by non–resident Indians living outside India in Indian owned banks. At the end of 1983, deposits held in U.S. dollar denominated, pound sterling denominated, and Indian rupee denominated accounts were $355 million, £109 million ($164 million), and Rs. 21,535 million ($2,153 million) respectively.[40] Such large levels of deposit maintenance in the external accounts, particularly in recent years, was facilitated by a two percentage point premium in the interest rate on those deposits over that on domestic deposits (Government of India, Ministry of Finance, 1984:63). This measure has proved so successful that there was acceleration in the accretion of deposits in these accounts from $285 million in 1981 to 1982 to $800 million in nine months of the fiscal year 1983 to 1984. The size of the deposit inflow was larger than private receipts under capital account of the balance of payments in 1981 to 1982 by about $70 million.[41]

Savings, Investment and Prices

The proportion of emigrants' savings actually remitted through official channels to India is not known. Weiner (1982) suggests that an Indian worker in the Middle East may remit to India one–third to one–half of his income. In the United Kingdom, Indian immigrants, on an average, saved 18 percent of their income and remitted to India only one–third of it (Rose 1969:194). Much of the savings of Indian immigrants in U.S. and Canada are invested in those countries because of the permanency of their settlement, presence of almost all nuclear family members in the household, and higher financial leverage available to them.[42] Besides funds sent through banking channels, they take some of their savings to India in the form of jewelry, cash and consumer durables which are sometimes sold to raise money for households. Black market dealings are also used to send money to the relatives.[43]

Emigrants' remittances (through official channels only) as a proportion of household savings in India has risen over 80 percent from 4.55 percent during the late 1970s to 8.25 percent during early 1980s. Such growth in remittances of emigrant households has improved their income, particularly in Kerala where remittances may account for as much as 15 percent of the personal income of all households.[44] Since many of the beneficiaries of remittances are from low–income rural households it might have reduced the inequality in income distribution.

Most of the funds received from abroad, particularly the Middle East, seemed to have been used in Kerala for consumption, purchase of agricultural land, construction of new houses, and education (Nair 1983:81-86). Only about 5 percent of the remittances have been invested in stocks, bonds and commercial enterprises.[45]

Heavy labor demand for construction activities at a time when such labor was migrating from Kerala to other countries has resulted in a substantial increase in wages for carpenters, masons, electricians, painters and laborers. Nair (1983) reports that wages of carpenters and masons almost quadrupled during 1973 to 1984 as against more than doubling of wholesale prices, suggesting a substantial increase in real wages for skilled workers in areas where emigration is concentrated. A large amount of cash available in the hands of emigrant households wanting to buy land, the supply of which is fixed, pushed land prices to a level 32 times higher than what it was in the mid 1970s.[46]

Conclusion

Indian emigration in modern times dates back to the late eighteenth century. Up to the first half of the twentieth century, about 3.1 million Indians might have migrated to different parts of the world. In the second half, 4.0 to 4.5 million people migrated to other countries. As of 1981 there were 5.0 to 5.5 million people born in India living in other countries, about 0.7 to 0.8 percent of the Indian population in 1981. The population of Indian origin living outside India is between 13.2 and 13.8 million which is catching up with the overseas Chinese population estimated to be between 15 and 20 million.

Indian migration before 1945 was mainly to neighboring countries (Ceylon, Burma and Malaya) and British sugar colonies (Fiji, Mauritius, and West Indies). After 1945, Nepal has become the foremost destination, followed by United Kingdom, United States and United Arab Emirates. Other major recipients of Indian immigrants are Canada, Kuwait, Libyan Arab Jamahiriya, Oman and Saudi Arabia.

Unlike the pre–1945 period dominated by poorly educated, agricultural laborers, the post–1945 period saw the emigration of highly educated persons. Excluding emigration to Nepal, for which no occupational composition of Indian immigrants is available, two out of nine Indian immigrants in the labor force of other countries are well qualified professionals such as doctors, engineers, scientists, administrators and professors. Four in nine comprise skilled technicians, sales and clerical persons and the rest are unskilled and semi-skilled workers and farm laborers. What is significant is that Indian emigration to developed countries consists mainly of professionals, and to developing countries is concentrated in other categories.

Age and sex characteristics of Indian emigrants seem to follow the general pattern of mainly young, male population in the beginning of the migration process and change to look similar to the one that prevails in the host country as the migration process "matures." The Indian immigrant population is generally much younger than other immigrant groups in receiving countries.

The major cause of emigration seems to be the wage differential between India and immigrant receiving countries. The desire to avoid professional isolation and to be independent, impatience with the slow rate of progress up the professional ladder in India, and an oversupply of trained people in certain fields are some of the other contributing causes for emigration from India.

The impact of emigration on population growth and birth rate decline was minimal, since the size of emigration from India in any one recent decade was only about 2 percent of the decennial population growth. Yet there seems to be an association between emigration and decline in rate of population growth on the one hand, and emigration and birth rate decline on the other, in major labor exporting states in India.

Emigration has certainly helped to ease the pressure on unemployment, particularly educated unemployment. The existence of a great reservoir of unemployed persons would lead one to conclude that emigration might not have created shortages of professionals, skilled and semi-skilled labor. However, the long run cost of "skill drain" to Indian society is likely to be high since the professional and technical emigrants constitute an elite human resource essential for development. Though emigration might have increased the productivity of those left behind in certain occupations, its net effect on Indian productivity is inconclusive.

Emigrants' remittances and deposits held in non–resident accounts in Indian owned banks have played a significant role in improving India's balance of payments position. The current account is strengthened considerably by the inflows of remittances which helped to finance an increasing proportion of merchandise trade deficit. This proportion was 53.4 percent in 1982. These remittances have grown so much that the total of $5,024 million during 1980 and 1981 exceeded the total foreign assistance utilized by $100 million.

The inflow of deposits in non-resident bank accounts fortified the capital account of the balance of payments. The size of this flow in 1981to 1982 was larger than the private receipts of $215 million by $70 million, and amounted to $800 million in nine months ending December, 1983.

The emigrants' remittances seemed to have contributed to the growth in household savings in India and accounted for 8.25 percent of the total household savings in 1980 to 1981. Besides improving the income of emigrant households enormously, in Kerala it seems to have contributed to the reduction of inequality in income distribution. However, these funds seem to have been utilized for investment in activities with low development priorities, such as expensive housing at inflated land and material prices.

Though emigration on the whole seems to have been beneficial to India, particularly in relieving the pressure of unemployment and in enabling the country to enjoy a comfortable foreign exchange reserve position, one cannot be certain about its long –term effects. What will the future of emigration in India be? Will it be beneficial or detrimental to India's development efforts? Should the government develop an active emigration policy? What steps should be taken to channel emigrants' remittances into more productive investments? These are some of the questions that will be raised in the future. With the information available now, answers to such questions can only be speculative. Unless steps are taken to fill the gaps in data, in-depth analyses for formulating emigration policies are difficult.

NOTES

1.   This exodus numbered at least 52 million people. See United Nations, Department of Economics and Social Affairs (1979:1). Also, during the same period, nearly 6 million Indians migrated to Burma, Sri Lanka, Malaysia, Fiji, Mauritius, Trinidad and Tobago, Guyana, Surinam, Jamaica, South Africa and East Africa.

2.   Data relating to the U.S. are from U.S. Department of Justice, Immigration Naturalization Service Statistical Yearbook, 1981 and that to Canada from Statistics Canada (1984).

3.   For foreign-born emigration from the U.S., see R. Warren and J. M. Beck (1980); for return migration from Australia, see C. A. Price (1981).

4.   Bohning (1984b:384) estimates the stock of migrant workers at the beginning of the 1980s at least 19.7 million to 21 million. After taking into account the omitted streams of foreign and undocumented worker movements, he wonders whether the global stock of migrant workers is nearer 25 million than 30 million. See also United Nations, Department of International Economic and Social Affairs (1982:69–94).

5.   See, for example, W. R. Bohning (1984a), J. H. Duloy (1967), A. N. E. Jolly (1971), K. Jones and A. Smith (1970), C. A. Price (1981), E. P. Reubens (1979), E. J. B. Rose et al. (1969), B. Thomas (1954, 1968), X. Zolotas (1966), and United Nations, Department of Social Affairs (1953).

6.   See for example Z. Baletic (1982), W. R. Bohning (1975), Fergany

(1982), T. Morrison and R. Sinkin (1982), E. J. B. Rose (1969), C. W. Stahl (1982), A. Songre (1973), World Bank (1979), P. R. Gopinathan Nair (1983), L. Gulati (1983), F. Arnold and N. M. Shah (1984), J. Power (1979), World Bank (1981), I. S. Gilani (1980), and J. S. Birks and C. A. Sinclair (1980).

7.   For a Typology of contemporary migration, see Bohning (1984a:47–60).

8.   See United Nations, Department of Economic and Social Affairs (1979:6–11) for a good discussion of statistical problems one encounters in the collection of migration data.

9.   India's relationship with neighboring countries goes back many centuries. For a historical account of the relationships before the nineteenth century between Malaya and India, see S. Arasaratnam (1970) and between Burma and India, see N. Chakravarti (1971). Among the Indian groups that went in search of wealth in Ceylon, Malaya and Burma, the most prominent community was *Nattukkottai Chettiars* or *Nagarathars*. According to H. Tinker (1977), they were the main bankers and traders of South India and Ceylon from medieval times. Gradually they extended their activities to Burma, Malaya, Thailand, Indo-China and Mauritius.

10.   See G. Omvedt (1980), P. Emmer (1984), and H. Tinker (1974).

11.   H. Tinker (1977:6).

12.   For an excellent discussion of the Kangani and non-Kangani systems of Labor Recruitment, see K. S. Sandhu (1969:87–102) and A. Bandarage (1983:203–215).

13.   The labor market was dominated by cash advances rather than wages. Planters preferred to compete for labor with offers of large cash advances instead of outright payment of higher wages. Unlike wages, cash advances tied the laborer to the plantation and ensured the planter his labor supply (C. D. Wesumperuma 1974, quoted in A. Bandarage).

14.   The *Nattukkottai Chettiars* or *Nagarattars*, in their role as a financial intermediary, seemed to have accumulated more wealth in Malaya, Burma, and Sri Lanka than any other Indian community.

15.   Indians were important economic actors in Burma. N. R. Chakravarti (1971: Chapter 7) estimates their wealth at somewhere between £150 and £375 million in 1938. This compared to a United Kingdom investment in Burma of £40 million to £50 million. The *Nattukkottai Chettiars'* wealth was assessed at £60 million. What was significant was that the latter group consisted of only about 1300 firms. It should, however, be noted that much of their wealth was nationalized and they did not receive any compensation.

16.   See D. P. Ghai and Y. S. Ghai (1970); K. Sandhu (1969); N. R. Chakravarti (1971).

17.   This must be taken with caution. Net immigration of estate labor into Ceylon during 1860 to 1890 was estimated at 710,000 by A. C. L. Ameer Ali (quoted by A. Bandarage). If this estimate is correct, then the number of Indians living outside India as of 1945 will be higher than 3.1 million.

18.   For example, the members of the *Nattukkottai Chettiar* community who left their womenfolk in their palatial homes in India will return to India every three years and spend two to three years in India. At the time of their return, it was customary to bring with them to India considerable amounts of money and jewelry for their womenfolk and children. A few of the large firms in this community initiated new industrial and commercial ventures in India.

19.   This estimate was given in a speech in Indian Parliament (see P. C. Jain, 1982).

20.   During 1962 to 1967, 42,440 Indian immigrants, most of whom were professionals and skilled people, and about 59,000 dependents arrived in United Kingdom (Rose 1969:85–86). The population of the United Kingdom born in India increased to 322,000 in April 1971 from 165,900 in April 1961 (United Nations, Department of Economics and Social Affairs, 1979:47).

21.   J. Ermish (1983:44).

22.   Estimates of overseas Indian population for various years are given in S. Nanjundan (1950), C. Kondapi (1951), K. Davis (1968), H. Tinker (1977) and P. C. Jain (1982). My estimate is higher than that of Jain by 1.1 to 1.7 million. Overseas Indian population has increased much more rapidly during the seventies and it is catching up with overseas Chinese population estimated between 15 and 20 million.

23.   Dr. Nallakrishnan of India, who has been involved in construction business in the Middle East for over a decade, said that unskilled workers would constitute 40 percent of Indian migrant labor force in Middle East; skilled workers, salespersons and clerks, 50 percent; and professionals and administrators, 10 percent.

24.   See United Nations, Department of International Economic and Social Affairs (1984:427–441).

25.   During 1965 to 1969, Indian immigrants accounted for less than 5 percent of professional, technical and workers who migrated to the U.S. This ratio reached its zenith in 1972 when one in six professionally and technically qualified immigrants was Indian. Since then it has shown a declining trend, with the average for the 1970s being 13.5.

26.   Estimated from data in U.S. Department of Justice, U.S. Immigration and Naturalization Annual Reports and statistical yearbooks, various issues.

27. It should be noted Indian students who came to Canada for higher studies are included. Estimates are based on data in Statistics Canada (1984).

28. For a theoretical analysis of the effects of emigration on economic development, see S. Friedlander (1965) and C. W. Stahl (1982).

29. In the 1960s, total emigration from India (including that to Nepal) was on the order of 2.4 million, and in the 1970s, 1.7 to 2.2 million. Indian population increased by 108 million during 1961 to 1971, and 136 million during 1971 to 1981.

30. Mr. A. Rahman, Director of National Institute of Science, Technology, and Development Studies, India is quoted in UNESCO 1984.

31. UNESCO 1984, *op. cit.*, p. 431.

32. Estimated from data relating to annual flow of graduates in scientific and technical fields given in Nair (1984).

33. UNESCO 1984, *op. cit.*, p. 430.

34. It is rather well known that no or slow growth in productivity in many factories, particularly public sector undertakings, are, in part, attributable to management deficiences.

35. Compare Swamy (1981:11) for trend rates of growth in remittances calculated for 30 countries which varied between 8.4 for Jamaica and 36.4 for Egypt. His estimate for India, covering the period 1967 to 1979, was 19.4.

36. International Monetary fund, International Financial Statistics, September 1984.

37. Emigrants' remittances from all countries excluding sterling area but including Canada averaged 408 million during 1975 to 1979, and $1,007 million during 1980 to 1981.

38. Average for 1980, 1981 and nine months of 1982.

39. See Government of India, Ministry of Finance 1984:152 for details on overall external assistance authorizations and utilizations. In 1978 to 1980, emigrants' remittances were equivalent to about 80 percent of foreign assistance utilized.

40. Estimates given under Rupee account include accrued interest. For more details, see Govt. of India, Ministry of Finance (1984:63).

41. This is the latest year for which data on private receipts are available.

42. In his study, G. Swamy (1981) reports some evidence for the hypothesis that per capita remittances decline as the migrant stays longer and his dependents in the host country increase and in the home country decline.

43.   See Nair (1983) and Arnold and Shah (1984).

44.   Nair (1983:69) states that "a substantial part of its per capita national (as against domestic) income, say about 15 percent, is considered to arise from remittances received from abroad."

45.   For comparison with other countries, see A. G. Chandavarkar (1980), I. S. Gilani (1980), J. Powers (1980), and Arnold and Shah (1984).

46.   Nair (1983) quotes Laurie Baker, "A spoiled child's toy blocks," *Indian Express*, May 22, 1983.

REFERENCES

Arasaratnam, S. (1970), *Indians in Malaya and Singapore* (Bombay: Oxford University Press, for the Institute of Race Relations).

Arnold, F., and Shah, N. M. (1984), "Asian Labor Migration to the Middle East," *International Migration Review*, Vol. XVIII, No. 2, pp. 294–317.

Aurora, G. S. (1967), *The New Frontiersmen* (Bombay: Popular Prakashan).

Baletic, Z. (1982), "International Migration in Modern Economic Development: With special reference to Yugoslavia," *International Migration Review*, Vol. XVI, No. 4, Winter, pp. 737–756.

Bandarage, A. (1983), *Colonialism in Sri Lanka: The Political Economy of the Kandyan Highlands, 1833–1886* (Berlin, New York & Amsterdam: Mouton).

Birks, J. S., and Sinclair, C. A. (1980), *International Migration and Development in the Arab Region* (Geneva: ILO).

Bohning, W. R. (1975), "Some Thoughts on Emigration from the Mediterranean Basin" Vol. III, No. 3, pp. 251–277.

Bohning, W. R. (1984a), *Studies in International Labour Migration* (New York: St. Martin's Press).

Bohning, W. R. (1984b), "International Migration: Implications for Development Policies" in United Nations, Dept. of International Economic and Social Affairs, *Population Distribution, Migration and Development*, pp. 379–403.

Boute, J. M. (1968), "Exploratory Analysis of Data Concerning Indians and Pakistanis in Africa," in J. C. Caldwell and C. Okanjo, (eds.), *The Population of Tropical Africa* (New York: Columbia University Press).

Butwel, R. (1972), "NE Win's Burma: At the End of the First Decade," *Asian Survey*, October.

Caribbean Year Book, 1979–80 (Toronto: Caribook).

Chakravarti, N. R. (1971), *The Indian Minority in Burma: The Rise and Decline of an Immigrant Community* (London).

Chandavarkar, A. G. (1980), "Use of Migrants' Remittances in Labor-Exporting Countries," *Finance and Development*, Vol. 17, No. 10, June.

Davis, K. (1968), *The Population of India and Pakistan* (New York: Russell and Russell).

Davison, R. B. (1962), *Black British* (London: Oxford University Press for Institute of Race Relations).

Desai, R. (1963), *Indian Immigrants in Britain* (London: Oxford University Press.

Duloy, J. H. (1967), "Structural Changes Due to Immigration: An Econometric Study," *Australian Economic Papers*, Vol. 6 (Dec.), pp. 223–233.

Emmer, P. (1984), "The Importation of British Indians into Surinam (Dutch Guiana), 1973–1916, in S. Marks, and P. C. Richardson, (Eds.), *International Labour Migration: Historical Perspectives* (London: Maurice Temple Smith published for the Institute of Commonwealth Studies), pp. 90–111.

Ermisch, J. (1983), *The Political Economy of Demographic Chance* (London: Heinaman).

Fergany, N. (1982), "The Impact of Immigration on National Development in the Arab Region: The Case of Yemen Arab Republic," *International Migration Review*, Vol. XVI, No. 4, Winter, pp. 757–780.

Friedlander, S. (1965), *Labor Migration and Economic Growth: A Case Study of Puerto Rico* (Cambridge, Massachusetts: The M.I.T. Press).

Ghai, D. S. and Ghai, Y. P. (1970), editors. *Portraits of a Minority* (London: Oxford University Press).

Gilani, I. S. (1980), *Preliminary Draft Report. Pakistani Emigration to the Middle-East, a Cost-Benefit Analysis*, Islamabad: Pakistan, Institute of Development Economics, July.

Gillian, K. L. (1962), *Fiji's Indian Migrants: A History to the End of Indenture in 1920* (Melbourne: Oxford University Press).

Government of Australia, *Yearbooks-Australia* (Various Issues).

Government of Canada, Statistics, Canada (1984), *Canada's Immigrants* (Ottawa; August).

Government of Canada, Immigration and Demographic Policy Group, *Immigration Statistics*, 1980 and 1981 Issues (Ottawa).

Government of India, Ministry of Finance (1984), *Economic Survey, 1983–84* (New Delhi: Government of India Press).

Government of India, Planning Commission (1969), *Fourth Five Year Plan, 1969–74-Draft* (New Delhi).

Government of India, Planning Commission (1978), *Draft Five Year Plan, 1978–83* (New Delhi).

Government of India, Planning Commission (1981), *Sixth Five Year Plan, 1980–85* (New Delhi).

Government of United Kingdom, Central Statistical Organization (1982) *Annual Abstract of Statistics, 1982* (London).

Government of United Kingdom, Central Statistical Organization (1984) *Regional Trends* (London).

Green, A. G. (1976), *Immigration and the Postwar Canadian Economy* (Toronto: Macmillan).

Gulati, L. (1983), "Impacts of Male Migration to the Middle East on the Family: Some Evidence from Kerala," *Economic and Political Weekly,* Vol. XVII, No. 52, December.

Hawkins, F. (1972), *Canada and Immigration* (Montreal: McGill-Queen's University Press).

Hill, C. (1970), Immigration and Integration (Oxford: Pergamon Press).

Horn, R. V. (1967), "Australia's Population," in S. Chandrasekhar (Ed), *Asia's Population Problems* (New York: Praeger).

International Monetary Fund (1984), *International Financial Statistics Yearbook, 1984* (Washington, D.C.).

International Monetary Fund, *Balance of Payments Yearbooks,* various issues.

Jain, P. C. (1982), "Indians Abroad: A Current Population Estimate," *Economic and Political Weekly,* Bombay, February 20, pp. 299–304.

Jolley, A. N. E. (1971), "Immigration and Australia's Postwar Economic Growth," *The Economic Record,* Vol. 47, No. 117, pp. 47–59.

Jones, K., and Smith, A. (1970), *The Economic Impact of Commonwealth Immigration* (London: Cambridge University Press for the National Institute of Economic and Social Research).

Kondapi, C. (1951), *Indians Overseas, 1838–1949* (Madras: Oxford University Press).

Kuczynski, R. R. (1948, 1949, 1953), *Demographic Survey of the British Colonial Empire,* 3 vol. (London: Oxford University Press).

Mishan, E. J. (1968), "Immigration: Some Long-term Economic Consequences," *Economia Internazionale,* Vol. XXI, Nos. 2 and 3, pp. 281–300 and 515–524.

Morrison, T., and Sinkin, R., "International Migration in the Dominican Republic—Implications for Development Planning," *International Migration Review,* Vol. XVI, No. 4, Winter, pp. 819–836.

Nair, P. R. Gopinathan (1983), *Asian Emigration to the Middle East: Emigration from India* (Trivandrum: Centre for Development Studies), Working Paper No. 180, November.

Nanjundan, S. (1950), *Indians in Malayan Economy* (New Delhi: Government of India, Office of Economic Registrar).

Nath, D. (1970), *A History of Indians in Guyana* (London: Published by the Author).

Omvedt, G. (1980), "Migration in Colonial India: The Articulation of Feudalism and Capitalism by the Colonial State," *The Journal of Peasant Studies,* Vol. 6, No. 2.

Overbeek, J. (1980), *Population and Canadian Society* (Butterworths).

Power, J. (1979), *Migrant Workers in Western Europe and the United States* (Oxford: Pergamon Press).

Price, C. A. (1981), "Long-Term Emigration and Immigration: A New Force in Australian International Movements," Paper Presented for the General Conference of the UISSP, Manila, Philippines, December.

Reserve Bank of India, *Report on Currency and Finance,* various issues.

Reubens, E. P. (1979), "International Migration Models and Policies," *American Economic Review,* Vol. 73, No. 2, pp. 178–182.

Rex, John, and Tomlinson, S. (1979), *Colonial Immigrants in a British City: A Class Analysis* (London: Routledge and Kegan Paul).

Rose, E. J. B. et al. (1969), *Colour and Citizenship: A Report on British Race Relations* (London: Oxford University Press for the Institute of Race Relations).

Sandhu, K. S. (1969), *Indians in Malaya: Some Aspects of Their Immigration and Settlement, 1786–1957* (London: Cambridge University Press).

Songre, A. (1973), "Mass Migration from Upper Volta: The Facts and Implications," *International Labour Review* (Geneva), Vol. 198, Nos. 2–3, pp. 209–225.

Stahl, C. W., "Labor Emigration and Economic Development," *International Migration Review,* Vol. XVI, No. 4, Winter, pp. 869–899.

Swamy, G. (1981), *International Migrant Workers' Remittances: Issues and Prospects* (Washington, D.C.: World Bank Staff Working Paper, No. 481, August).

Swee-Hock, S. (1970), *Singapore: Population in Transition* (Philadelphia: University of Pennsylvania Press).

Tandon, Y. (1973), *Problems of a Displaced Minority: The New Position of East Africa's Asians* (London: Minority Rights Group, Report No. 16).

Thomas, B. (1954), Migration and Economic Growth (Cambridge: Cambridge University Press).

Thomas, B. (1968), "Migration II: Economic Aspects," in *International Encyclopedia of Social Sciences,* Vol. 10, D. L. Shils, ed. (London and Glencoe) pp. 292–300.

Tinker, H. (1977), *The Banyon Tree: The Overseas Immigrant from India, Pakistan and Bangladesh* (Oxford: Oxford University Press).

United Nations (1977), *Demographic Year Book, 1977* (New York: United Nations).

United Nations, *Monthly Bulletin of Statistics,* various issues (New York: United Nations).

United Nations, Department of Economic and Social Affairs (1979), *Trends and Characteristics of International Migration Since 1950* (New York: United Nations).

United Nations, Department of Interntional Economic and Social Affairs (1982), *World Population Trends and Policies: 1981 Monitoring Report,* Vol. II, *Population Policies* (New York: United Nations).

United Nations, Department of Social Affairs, Population Division (1953), *The Determinants and Consequences of Population Trends,* Population Study, No. 17 (New York: United Nations).

United Nations Educational, Scientific, and Cultural Organization (1984), "Brain Drain or the Migration of Talent and Skills," in U.N. Dept. of International Economic and Social Affairs, *Population Distribution, Migration and Development,* pp. 427–441.

United Nations, International Labor Organization (1984), *Bulletin of Labor Statistics, Third Quarter* (Geneva).

United Nations, International Labor Organization (1983), *Yearbook of Labor Statistics* (Geneva).

U.S. Department of Commerce, Bureau of the Census (1984), *Statistical Abstract of the United States, 1984* (Washington, D.C.).

U.S. Department of Justice, Immigration and Naturalization Service, *Annual Reports,* various issues (Washington, D.C.: U.S. Government Printing Office).

U.S. Department of Justice, Immigration and Naturalization Service, *Statistical Yearbooks of the Immigration and Naturalization Service, 1978 through 1981* (Washington, D.C.).

Warren, R. and Peck, M. M. (1980), "Foreign-Born Emigration from the United States, 1900–1970," *Demography*, Vol. 17, No. 1, Feb., pp. 71–84.

Weiner, M. (1978), *Sons of the Soil: Migration and Ethnic Conflict in India* (Princeton, New Jersey: Princeton University Press).

Weiner, M. (1982), "International Migration and Development" *Population and Development Review*, Vol. 8, No. 1, March.

Whelan, J. (1974), "Brain Drain: A Study of the Persistent Issue of International Scientific Mobility" (Washington, D.C.).

Wilcox, W. F. (1929), *International Migrations: Volt Statistics* (New York: National Bureau of Economic Research).

World Bank (1979), *World Development Report* (Washington, D.C.).

World Bank (1981), *Labor Migration from Bangladesh to the Middle East* (Washington, D.C., World Bank Staff Working Paper No. 454).

Zolotas, X. (1966), *International Labor Migration and Economic Development* (Athens: Bank of Greece).

TABLE 1
ESTIMATES OF POPULATION BORN IN INDIA
AND OF INDIAN ORIGIN IN SELECTED
COUNTRIES, 1981 (000s)

Country	Total Population	Population Born in India	Indian Origin	Indian Origin as % of Total
Australia	14,930	33	35	0.23
Bahrain	360	23–47	24–50	6.66–13.89
Burma	35,100	50	1,050	2.99
Canada	24,300	110	140	0.58
Ethiopia	32,750	n.a.	5	0.02
Fiji	650	n.a.	325	50.00
Grenada	110	NIL	4	4.00
Guyana	880	neg	449	51.02
Hong Kong	5,150	12	14	0.27
Indonesia	153,850	neg	40	0.03
Iraq	13,670	4–44	4–44	0.03–0.32
Jamaica	2,200	neg	44	2.00

Country	Total Population	Population Born in India	Indian Origin	Indian Origin as % of Total
Kenya	17,340	20	100	0.58
Kuwait	1,470	65–155	67–120	4.56–10.33
Laos	4,000	NIL	2	0.05
Libya Arab Jamahiriya	3,100	71–87	72–88	2.32–2.84
Madagaskar	8,960	n.a.	15	0.17
Malawi	6,110	n.a.	15	0.25
Malaysia	14,200	350	1,200	8.45
Mauritius	940	n.a.	649	69.00
Nepal	15,020	2,780	3,200	21.30
Nigeria	83,310	20	20	0.02
Oman	910	50–94	53–97	5.82–10.66
Philippines	49,540	n.a.	4	0.01
Qatar	260	20–43	21–44	8.07–16.92
Saudi Arabia	9,630	66–182	68–184	0.71–1.91
Singapore	2,440	51	164	6.72
South Africa	29,300	n.a.	800	2.73
Sri Lanka	14,990	234	2,770	18.48

TABLE 1 (Continued)
ESTIMATES OF POPULATION BORN IN INDIA AND OF INDIAN ORIGIN IN SELECTED COUNTRIES, 1981 (000s)

Country	Total Population	Population Born in India	Indian Origin	Indian Origin as % of Total
Surinam	360	neg	133	36.90
Tanzania	19,160	5	50	0.26
Thailand	47,490	n.a.	25	0.05
Trinidad and Tobago	1,110	neg	440	39.63
United Arab Emirates	1,060	180–420	195–444	18.40–41.89
United Kingdom	56,350	420	500	0.89
United States	229,850	194	410	0.18
Yemen Arab Republic	5,300	4–5	4–5	0.08–0.09
Zaire	29,380	4	5	0.02
Zambia	5,830	8	10	0.17
Zimbabwe	7,360	8	10	0.14
Others	—	110	120	—

Notes
1. Total population estimates are from United Nations, Monthly Bulletin of Statistics, August 1984.

2. Population born in India, where necessary, was estimated using a balancing equation.

3. "neg" indicates less than 1,000, "n.a." indicates that information is not available.

4. "Others" include western Europe (excluding the U.K.), Japan, New Zealand, Iran, Jordan, South Yemen, Sudan, Somalia, Egypt, Aden, Mexico, and Brazil.

Sources of Data
Australia: 1) Yearbook, Australia, various issues; 2) R.V. Horn 1969:225; 3) United Nations, Dept of Economics and Social Affairs 1979:56. Immigrant (settlers arriving) data are used here. About 15,000 people who claimed India as their former country of residence have become citizens of Australia during July 1945–June 1975.

Burma: 1) A Yearbook of the Commonwealth 1980; 2) personal communication from Dr. Krishan Bharadwaja; 3) R. Butwel 1972:901–08; 4) K.S. Sandhu 1969:61 and 157 5) Tinker 1977.

Canada: 1) F. Hawkins 1972:58; 2) A. Green 1976; 3) United Nations, Dept of Economics and Social Affairs 1979:48; 4) Statistics Canada 1984. People of Indian descent born outside of India are not included here.

Ethiopia: 1) P.C. Jain 1982:303.

Fiji: 1) A Yearbook of the Commonwealth 1980; 2) Gillion 1962:207. Indian immigrants were entering Fiji as late as the 1960's but only in very small numbers.

Grenada: 1) R.R. Kuczynski 1953:398–99; 2) A Yearbook of the Commonwealth, 1980.

Guyana: 1) D. Nath 1970:219–20; 2) R.R. Kuczynski 1953:12.

Hong Kong: 1) A Yearbook of the Commonwealth; 2) Tinker 1977:12.

Philippines, Indonesia, Laos, Nepal, Thailand: 1) P.C. Jain
1982:300–03.

*Bahrain, Kuwait, Iraq, Libya, Oman, Qatar, Saudi Arabia,
United Arab Emirates:*   1) W.R. Bohning 1984:22; 2) R.
Thomas 1982:49; 3) Tinker 1977:12. The lower bound
estimate of people of Indian origin in these countries is based
on the estimates of number of workers in Bohning, cited
above, and the upper bound was derived by applying
participation rates to an estimate of 599,500 workers in the
Persian Gulf region in March 1981, which was given by the
external affairs minister from the Indian parliament. In May
1983 another Indian minister visiting this area said that there
were one million workers in these countries. See G. Nair
(1983). These estimates may include undocumented Indians
living in these countries.

Jamaica: 1) Kuczynski 1953:235–36; 2) Caribbean Yearbook
1980.

Kenya, Tanzania: 1) J.M. Boute 1968:242; 2) H.S. Chhabra
1981:51; 3) D.P. Ghai and Y.S. Ghai 1970; 4) N. Monstead and
Walji 1978: 146; 5) Tinker 1977:119. Estimates refer to Indians
and Pakistanis.

Madagaskar: 1) Tinker 1977:12; 2) P.C. Jain 1982:303. Figures
relate to South Asians.

Malawi: J.M. Boute 1968:247.
Malaysia: 1) K.S. Sandhu 1969:304–317; 2) A Yearbook of the
Commonwealth 1980, 3) United Nations, Demographic
Yearbook 1977: Table 24.

Mauritius: 1) Kuczynsky 1949:797; 2) A Yearbook of the
Commonwealth 1980.

Nigeria: 1) A Yearbook of the Commonwealth 1980. The total
non-African population was estimated in 1981 at less than
40,000; 2) Tinker (1977:12) estimated the South Asian
population in 1970–71 at 1,600.

Singapore: 1) Swee-Hock 1980:17 and 213. Data relate to
Indian, Pakistani and Sri Lankan origins.

Surinam: 1) P. Emmer 1984:99; 2) Caribbean Yearbook 1980.

Trinidad, Tobago: Kuczynski 1953:12 and 14.

United Kingdom: 1) E.J.B. Rose and Assoc. 1969; 2) C. Hill 1970:27; 3) Central Statistical Office, Regional Trends 1984; 4) Central Statistical Office, Annual Abstract of Statistics, 1982, 1983:26. Data exlude "white" Indians.

United States: 1) U.S. Dept of Justice, Annual Report, Immigration and Naturalization Service, various issues.

Zambia, Zimbabwe: 1) J.M. Boute 1969:247–49; 2) A Yearbook of the Commonwealth 1980. Data relate to Asians.

TABLE 2
ESTIMATES OF NET INDIAN MIGRANT FLOWS, SELECTED COUNTRIES, 1800–1980
(000s)

Country	Up to 1920	1921–45	1946–60	1961–70	1971–80
Australia	NIL	....	3	26[a]	5[a]
Bahrain	—	1	1	5	16–40
Burma	n.a.	618[b]	c	c	c
Canada	5	—	3	28	75
Fiji	69	n.a.	n.a.	n.a.	—
Guyana	173	–5	—	—	—
Hong Kong	n.a.	n.a.	1	10	1
Iraq	—	1	—	9[d]	30
Jamaica	7	—	—	—	—
Kenya, Tanzania, Uganda	40	80	86	c	c
Kuwait	—	1	—	17[d]	47–97
Libya Arab Jamahiriya	—	—	—	—	71–87
Malaysia	744	377	80	63	20
Mauritius	300	n.a.	n.a.	n.a.	n.a.

Country	Up to 1920	1921–45	1946–60	1961–70	1971–80
Nepal	n.a.	n.a.	70	1920	800
Nigeria	—	—	—	—	20[e]
Oman	n.a.	1	1	2	46–90
Qatar	n.a.	n.a.	n.a.	3	17–40
Saudi Arabia	—	—	—	1	66–182
Singapore	[f]	[f]	—	51[d]	[c]
Surinam	57	...	—	—	—
Trinidad and Tobago	109	−5	—	—	—
United Arab Emirates	n.a.	n.a.	n.a.	n.a.	180–420
United Kingdom[g]	n.a.	31	33	201	97
United States	7	3	3	27	164

[a] 1961–70 data refer to 1960–73, and 1971–80 to 1974–80.

[b] According to the 1931 census there were 618,000 Indians in Burma who were born in India.

[c] Net migration was substantially negative, but reliable data are not available.

[d] Includes net migration during some years in the previous period.

[e] Refers to 1961–80. It is about one-half of the total non-African population in Nigeria.

[f] Included in Malaysia.

[g] Excludes "white" Indians (children of British parents born in India, retired population and repatriates since 1947).

" . . . " indicates negligible numbers.

SOURCES: Same as in Table 1.

TABLE 3
COMPOSITION OF INDIAN IMMIGRANTS ADMITTED INTO THE U.S.
BY MAJOR OCCUPATION GROUPS

Occupation Group	1964–79	%	1975–79	%	1970–74	%	1965–69	%
Professional, technical and kindred workers	66,774	37.5	26,742	29.1	30,638	45.6	9,174	50.3
Administrators (except farm)	5,494	3.1	4,055	4.4	1,171	1.7	252	1.4
Sales, clerical, craft and operatives	10,001	5.6	6,209	6.8	2,844	4.2	869	4.8
Laborers, service, household and farm laborers	3,798	2.1	2,614	2.8	838	1.2	311	1.7
Housewives, children and others with no occupation	91,938	51.6	52,358	56.9	31,661	47.1	7,635	41.9
Total	178,005	100.0	91,978	100.0	67,152	100.0	18,241	100.0

Based on data in the various issues of annual reports of the Immigration and Naturalization Service, Department of Justice, U.S. Government.

TABLE 4
COMPOSITION OF U.S. NATURALIZED CITIZENS WITH FORMER ALLEGIANCE
TO INDIA BY MAJOR OCCUPATION GROUP

Occupational Group	1964–79	%	1975–79	%	1970–74	%	1965–69	%
Professional technical and kindred workers	24,089	54.2	6,732	48.8	13,802	56.7	2,785	60.0
Managers and administrators (except farm)	2,677	6.0	900	6.5	1,408	5.8	230	5.0
Sales, clerical, craft, and operatives	5,332	12.0	1,973	14.3	2,855	11.7	340	7.3
Laborers, service, household and farm laborers	1,770	4.0	666	4.8	725	3.0	278	6.0
Housewives, children and others with no occupation	10,516	23.7	3,504	25.4	5,546	22.8	1,013	21.8
Total	44,473	100.0	13,785	100.0	24,326	100.0	4,645	100.0

SOURCE: Same as in Table 3.

TABLE 5
ESTIMATES OF INDIAN IMMIGRANTS BY OCCUPATION IN SELECTED COUNTRIES OR REGIONS, 1981

Category	United States	United Kingdom	Australia	Canada	Western Europe	West Asia	Malaysia	Singapore	Hong Kong	Nigeria
Number of immigrants	194,000	380,000	33,000	110,000	75,000	950,000	350,000	51,000	12,000	20,000
Proportion in labor force	48.4	42.0	48.4	42.0	48.4	63.1	47.9	49.0	41.7	45.0
Number in labor force	94,000	160,000	16,000	46,000	36,000	599,500	167,500	25,000	5,000	9,000
Professional technical and kindred workers	72,800	24,000	12,400	24,200	27,900	54,000	10,000	2,000	500	5,000
Managers and administrators	6,100	1,500	1,000	2,300	2,300	5,500	2,500	500	100	—
Sales, clerical, craft and operatives	11,000	80,000	1,900	16,000	4,200	300,000	60,000	10,000	3,000	1,000
Laborers and service workers	4,100	54,500	700	3,500	2,600	240,000	95,000	12,500	1,900	3,000

Estimated on the basis of sources referred to in Table 1.

TABLE 6
COMPOSITION OF INDIAN IMMIGRANTS BY OCCUPATION
AND ITS RELATIONSHIP TO UNEMPLOYMENT LEVEL IN 1981
AND GROWTH IN UNEMPLOYMENT DURING 1974–81

Occupation	Developed Countries	Developing Countries	Total	Number Unemployed in India	Growth in Unemployment
Professional, technical and kindred workers	161,300	71,500	232,800	836,000	393,000
Managers and administrators	13,200	8,600	21,800	10,000	1,000
Sales, clerical, craft and operatives	113,100	374,000	487,100	2,427,000	993,000
Laborers and service workers	65,400	352,400	417,800	13,983,000[a]	7,849,000[a]

First three columns are derived from estimates in Table 5. Fourth and fifth columns are estimated from data in United Nations, International Labor Organization 1983:467.

[a] Does not include unemployed agricultural laborers.

TABLE 7
DAILY STATUS UNEMPLOYED RATES BY STATES
1972–73 and 1977–78

State/Union Territory	1972–73	1977–78
Kerala	25.23	25.69
Pondicherry	17.86	22.62
Tamilnadu	12.17	15.59
Goa	18.97	14.63
Delhi	5.47	10.96
Andhra Pradesh	12.01	10.67
West Bengal	10.66	10.15
Karnataka	9.20	9.36
Orissa	10.82	8.13
Bihar	10.24	8.01
Maharastra	9.73	7.99
Haryana	4.10	6.41
Gujarat	6.36	6.24
Jammu and Kashmir	8.38	5.70
Tripura	6.41	5.04
Chandigarh	neg	4.94
Punjab	4.54	4.82
Uttar Pradesh	3.68	4.12
Madhya Pradesh	3.67	3.09
Rajasthan	3.72	2.99
Manipur	5.14	2.00
Himachal Pradesh	0.82	1.92
Assam	1.98	1.81
Nagaland	neg	1.03
Meghalaya	1.82	0.41
Arunachal Pradesh	—	0.35
All India	8.34	8.18

SOURCES: Government of India, Planning Commission, *Sixth Five Year Plan,*
1980–85, New Delhi, p. 216, and *Draft Five Year Plan, 1978–83,* New
Delhi, p. 94.

TABLE 8

ESTIMATES OF ECONOMICALLY ACTIVE POPULATION AMONG EDUCATED PERSONS, UNEMPLOYED PERSONS AND IMPLIED UNEMPLOYMENT RATE, 1980 AND 1985

Category	Economically Active Population (000s)			Unemployed Persons (000s)		Implied Unemployment Rate
	1980	1985	Increase	1980	1985	
Engineering graduates	221	266	45	16	19	7.1
Engineering diploma holders	329	430	101	66	86	19.9
Medical graduates	155	184	29	10	12	6.5
Dental graduates	10	12	2	negligible		2.0
Nursing graduates	2	3	1	n.a.	n.a.	n.a.
Agricultural science graduates	77	90	13	9	10	11.4
Veterinary science graduates	19	24	4	1	1	3.6
Education graduates	665	910	245	104	143	15.7
Arts and humanities graduates	1,506	2,026	520	338	455	22.4
Basic science graduates	750	957	206	154	197	20.6
Commerce graduates	632	878	246	111	155	17.6
Post-graduates, arts and humanities	747	1,011	264	30	40	4.0

TABLE 8 (Continued)
ESTIMATES OF ECONOMICALLY ACTIVE POPULATION AMONG EDUCATED PERSONS, UNEMPLOYED PERSONS AND IMPLIED UNEMPLOYMENT RATE, 1980 AND 1985

Category	Economically Active Population (000s)			Unemployed Persons (000s)		Implied Unemployment Rate
	1980	1985	Increase	1980	1985	
Post-graduates, basic sciences	218	273	56	11	13	4.9
Post-graduates, commerce	95	138	42	6	9	6.5
Other graduates	975	1,290	316	154	316	15.8
Total graduates and above, including diploma holders	6,403	8,492	2,090	1,009	1,343	15.8
Matriculates and higher secondary school graduates	16,257	21,875	5,618	2,463	3,314	15.2
Total educated persons	22,660	30,367	7,708	3,472	4,657	15.3

Data refer to the beginning of 1980 and 1985.
Includes post graduates.
"n.a." indicates data not available.

SOURCE: Government of India, Planning Commission, Sixth Five Year Plan, 1980–85, New Delhi, p. 220.

TABLE 9
ESTIMATES OF STOCK OF EDUCATED PERSONS,
SELECTED YEARS (000s)

Category	1960–61	1968–69	1980	1985
Engineering graduates	58	134	225	306
Engineering diploma holders	75	198	379	494
Medical graduates	70	102	179	212
Nursing graduates	n.a.	n.a.	2	3
Dental graduates	n.a.	n.a.	12	13
Agricultural science graduates	14	48	99	116
Veterinary science graduates	5	12	22	27
Education graduates	n.a.	n.a.	853	1,137
Arts and humanities graduates	n.a.	n.a.	1,931	2,598
Basic science graduates	n.a.	n.a.	962	1,226
Commerce graduates	n.a.	n.a.	810	1,126
Post graduates, arts and humanities	n.a.	n.a.	957	1,296
Post graduates, basic sciences	n.a.	n.a.	279	350
Post graduates, commerce	n.a.	n.a.	122	176
Other graduates	n.a.	n.a.	1,250	1,654
Total graduates and above, including diploma holders	n.a.	n.a.	8,110	10,735
Matriculate/higher secondary school graduates	n.a.	n.a.	26,650	35,860
Total educated persons	n.a.	n.a.	34,760	46,595

Columns 1 and 2 refer to fiscal year ending March 31. Columns 3 and 4 to January 1 of each year.

SOURCES: Government of India Planning Commission, *Sixth Five Year Plan, 1980–85*, p. 220 and *Fourth Five Year Plan, 1969–74* (Draft), pp. 291–293.

TABLE 10
PRIVATE UNREQUITTED TRANSFER FLOWS INTO INDIA AND THEIR RELATIONSHIP TO EXPORTS, BALANCE OF TRADE, AND BALANCE ON GOODS AND SERVICES, 1960–81
(ANNUAL AVERAGES, MILLIONS OF U.S. DOLLARS)

Period (1)	Private Unrequitted Transfers (2)	Exports (3)	Trade Balance (4)	Balance on Goods and Services (5)	Column (2) as % of		
					(3)	(4)	(5)
1980–81	2,512 (1,505)	8,370	−5,763	−5,517	30.0	43.6	45.5
1975–79	909 (461)	6,088	−335	−466	14.9	271.3	195.1
1970–74	131 (70)	2,547	−296	−774	5.1	44.3	16.9
1965–69	137	1,700	−650	−1,094	7.7	20.2	12.0
1960–64	78	1,490	−692	−954	5.2	11.2	8.1

Private unrequitted transfers exclude credits in lieu of contra-entries for imports from the U.S. under P.L. 480 (Titles II and III), but includes unilateral transfers like maintenance remittances and receipts of missionaries.

Numbers in parentheses refer to transfers from sterling area (excluding Canada) countries and relate to fiscal years rather than calendar years.

Based on data in International Monetary Fund, International Financial Statistics-1984 Yearbook and Reserve Bank of India, Report on Currency and Finance (various issues).

CHAPTER 4

ECONOMIC IMPACT OF EUROPEAN MIGRATION TO LATIN AMERICA AFTER WORLD WAR II

Norman Plotkin

It has been estimated that over the past 150 years, roughly twelve million people have moved to Latin America. Of these, about four million were of Spanish descent, four million were Italian and about two million were Portuguese. There were also small groups of Germans and Poles. These European immigrants tended to concentrate in the few countries where the economic opportunities seemed most promising. The two countries dominant in attracting the mass of immigrants were Brazil and Argentina. It is these on which we will mainly draw for evidence in this study.[1]

This long period of European immigration to Latin America essentially reflects two major waves. The first was from the latter half of the nineteenth century to the 1920s, or the so–called "big boom" period. This was followed by a period of immigration lull in the late 1920s and 1930s due to rising nationalism and then the economic depression. The second wave took place from the end of World War II to the middle of the 1950s, overlapping in some cases, into the early 1960s. These waves appear to be very different both in terms of their size and duration, the type of immigrant and his expectations, and the evidence of its economic impact.

The greatest mass movement took place during the first wave. This was at a time when the populations of Latin American countries were relatively small so that the number of immigrants made a substantial impact on the growth, structure and culture of the population.[2] The literature for this period is rich with the evidence of the demographic, social, cultural and economic contributions these immigrants and their descendants have made in Argentina and Brazil.[3]

On the other hand, the literature on the economic effect of post World War II Europeans is much leaner and the evidence more conjectural. The numbers of immigrants absorbed, relative to the population of Argentina and Brazil, were relatively small in percentage and the consensus appears to be that their demographic impact was slight. They also appear to have been largely selected by the receiving countries based on a previous vision of immigrant use inappropriate to this generation of Europeans who were a different breed. If these immigrants were to make a substantial economic impact, the major reason would not be due to their numbers but rather to the nature of the immigrants themselves—their values, drive or difference in outlook that gave them an entrepreneurial edge over the native population. It is his hypothesis the author will also explore based upon the evidence available.

The Potential Economic Effects of Immigration

It would seem useful as an initial structure for analysis to list the effects one might expect from a substantial immigration on a developing country receiving them, as in the Latin American case. Immigration may:[4]

1.   Modify the structure of the country's population if the immigrants differ significantly from the native population.

2.   Accelerate the rate of population growth if its size, relative to the population size, is large.

3.   Increase the country's aggregate income as the immigrants add to the labor force, to the extent they do not replace native workers.

4.   Increase the labor force at a rate greater than population growth if, as is usual, an abnormally large fraction of the immigrants is of working age.[5]

5.   Increase in the country's aggregate income per capita if the immigrant serves to release the forces of increasing returns by introducing new and superior skills and new sets of values important to entrepreneurial activity and industrial productivity.

6.   Improve the possibility for developing import–competitive industries.

7.   Stimulate foreign investment by offering a skill and quantity level of manpower that might make such investment seem attractive.

8.   Cause shifts in occupational emphasis as immigrants tend to emphasize and dominate certain occupations and industries causing internal substitution effects with the native labor force.

9.   Generate inflation and forced savings in the process of trying to equip immigrants with residential and industrial capital.

Pre–World War II Immigration Wave

In pre–World War II immigration to Argentina, up to 6.5 million immigrants were admitted: three million from Italy, two million from Spain and others from Germany and East–Central Europe. They were offered incentives of assisted passage, quick citizenship and exemption from military service. By 1900, a quarter of the Argentina population was foreign born.[6] It was this group of mainly unskilled farm laborers that transformed the Pampa and Argentina into a major world food producing and exporting area.

Brazil, in turn, received more than 4 million European immigrants between 1887 and 1936. These were comprised mainly of Italians (1,354,000), Portuguese (1,147,000), Spaniards (577,000), Germans (155,000) and Russians (107,000).[7] These large numbers of relatively young Europeans played an important part in Brazil's economic development; but perhaps not in the way they had originally intended when they migrated to Brazil.

The mass of immigrants and their social and economic impacts on both countries were important factors in setting the immigration pattern and views in the post–World War II wave. As a prelude to that, an examination of their economic effects, using Brazil as the main example, would seem to be useful.

Brazil: The Economic Impact of the First Wave

For Brazil the period from 1880 through the 1900s was one of dynamic economic change. Expansion of coffee growing became the critical instrument of this change. São Paulo became the dominant Brazilian economic region powered by "an explosive burst of externally induced investment activity," mainly from Great Britain.[8] Some indices of this growth are shown in Table I.[9]

TABLE 1
BRAZIL: INDICES OF ECONOMIC GROWTH
1880–1929 (OR 1930)

Productive Factors	1880	1914	1929 (or 1930)
Population (millions)	11.7	23.7*	37.4
Railway lines	3,400 km.	24,600 km.	32,000 km.
Electric power capacity	negligible	152,000 K.W.*	700,000 K.W.
Value of exports (000s)	£21,000	£65,000	£95,000
Foreign capital outstanding	$190 million	$1.9 billion	$2.6 billion

* In 1910

The upswing in world demand for coffee which resulted in Brazilian coffee expansion was coincidental with the abolition of slave labor in Brazil (1888) and a shortage of agricultural labor. European immigrant manpower was sought as a substitute for this slave labor and the growing coffee profits were used to subsidize the effort to obtain European immigration.[10]

The more than four million European immigrants were mainly landless and unskilled farm laborers. They were enticed largely by the "open spaces" picture painted of Brazil and the dream of becoming a property owner. If their dream was to become independent farmers, few fulfilled that dream because Brazil, as was also the case in Argentina, was dominated by large estates and the great landowners occupied the most sought after land.

De Avila notes that the immigrants were largely reduced to wage–earning farm workers, which seems to have been the intent of the coffee planters in São Paulo and the great cattle raisers of the south.[11] This may account for the large re–emigration of Italians. Merrick and Graham noted that from 1902 to 1913, over 200,000 Italians returned to Italy from Brazil and 400,000 from Argentina.[12] Spengler notes that the percentage of net to gross immigrants was 54 percent in Argentina in the period 1857 to 1948, and 74 percent in Brazil in the period 1872 to 1940.[13] Yet, a critical factor in their favor was the sharp upswing in Brazilian growth in the 1880s which increased the immigrant's bargaining power.

The European immigrant was generally a much different breed of workman—more ambitious and more productive—than the native Brazilian workers. De Avila ascribes to "the typical Brazilian peasant . . . a philosophy of life to which the notion of progress and of economic profit is foreign." He has "learned to be content with winning from nature the barest necessities and, due to consequent fatalism, has little ambition to improve his condition."[14]

Contrasted to this, the European immigrants came from a more advanced industrial culture. Most were in their full productive years and had acquired some education in their mother countries. De Avila estimates that the value of human capital resulting from the immigration, if borne internally by Brazil, was about 49 billion Crs., or substantially more than its national income in 1939 (40 billion Crs.).[15] They brought with them new attitudes, new skills and new perceptions. Blocked in one area many tended to seek success in agriculturally related or non–agricultural pursuits. Many ended up flowing to the cities, organizing new commercial and industrial enterprises and providing a core of skilled workers and foremen.

Merrick and Graham, in examining comparative literacy of native–born and foreign–born in the 1900 to 1940 period, concluded that the latter had a much stronger human resource base.[16] Interestingly, they note this was in sharp contrast to the situation in the United States. There it was the native–born who registered the much higher level of literacy and educational status. It would seem that the European immigrants that flowed to Latin America brought a skill and human capital capability generally superior to that of the native–born in these developing countries while the

reverse was true of the United States.[17] Merrick and Graham claim
that these immigrants acted as

> "important catalysts in extending [Brazilian] growth into broader
> multisectoral paths than would have occurred without their pres-
> ence as laborers and entrepreneurs . . . their economic participa-
> tion helped to create new jobs through the expansion of the
> economy (which they then filled in the industrial and commercial
> sectors) rather than displacing natives from established occupa-
> tions."[18]

The European immigrant, as a farm laborer, took advantage of
the opportunities provided by the "colona" labor system in the
Paulista coffee sector, which offered rent–free housing, near
self–sufficiency in food production and a variety of sources of
income. This afforded opportunities for saving and mobility
which many eventually used to buy small parcels of land or to
migrate to urban areas and set up a new situation, thereby "rising
above their earlier poverty" and escaping exploitation "as conve-
nient substitutes for slave labor."[19]

Through this accumulation and business acumen, the original
immigrant (and his descendants) gradually built up small and
medium sized coffee tree farms (but not large) so that, by 1932,
almost 40% of the coffee trees in Western São Paulo were owned
by foreign born.[20] As the urban industrial section expanded to
service the coffee economy during this period, the evidence
appears to be clean that many of the European immigrants were
ready to take over an entrepreneurial role.[21]

Bakalanoff noted various studies showing the industrial dominance of immigrant stock in São Paulo as well as other states of
Brazil. He concluded:

> "The evidence seems pretty strong that it was the immigrants and
> their descendants who most effectively perceived the industrial
> opportunities which followed from the coffee prosperity, the rail-
> road boom and the growth of urban centers. The immigrants were a
> decisive factor in Brazil's incipient industrial revolution."[22]

While the European "entrepreneurial" sense and ambition
appear present in the efforts of the initial immigrants, some
question has been raised whether the interaction of cultures
didn't make a change in the immigrants' descendants as they were
absorbed into the prevailing value system and the less competitive way of life of the country. This view holds that the native

Brazilian entrepreneur was unwilling to take risks and this same attitude was instilled in the descendants of these European immigrants. Instead, this implies, it was the state that was required to be the risk taker. Cardoso paints a picture of the middle class entrepreneurial groups as unwilling to take responsibility for industrial development except under the protection of the state. They would act only after public investment and opened new sources of profit for import substitutes with the market for these protected by state measures which benefited the industrialist.[23]

Post–World War II Immigration Wave

In the aftermath of World War II there was a deep surge in European emigration estimated to be similar in gross volume to its 1880–1900 emigration period.[24] The migrants in this movement were of two very different types.

1.   Millions of refugees and displaced persons, many highly skilled, were seeking a new country to start their lives. The International Refugee Organization (IRO) was formed to help these migrants resettle.

2.   "Voluntary" migrants who represented an excess supply of labor to the post–war deteriorated economies of European countries, such as Italy. The International Committee for European migration estimated that there were five million surplus people in Europe.[25]

The estimates of the size of migrants from Europe to receiving countries differ according to the study and source, but the general size of the movement appears to be in agreement and sufficient for this study. By the middle of the 1950s, the main force of migration began to decline as European economic recovery took hold and offered more attractive alternatives nearer home to most Europeans. In the Appendix, immigration statistics have been drawn from various sources as reference.

Kirk and Huyck, after compiling European migration data from various sources, concluded that "the net identifiable outward movement" of European emigrants for the period 1946-1952 was 3.2 million.[26] Based upon a more conservative figure of 2.2 million net identifiable immigrants, they estimated that Latin America received and held 823,000 in this period as follows (in 000's):[27]

Spanish American Receiving Country	Net Migrant	Sending Countries			
		Italy	Portugal	Spain	Other*
Argentina	489	314	7	141	27
Brazil	174	49	95	6	24
Venezuela	86	61	7	13	5
Other	74*	17	2	18	37

*Primarily Netherlands to Surinam, Italy to Uruguay and Peru, and Spain to Cuba

Robbins' estimate of net migration from Europe to the Americas was higher than Kirk and Huyck at 2.4 million with 60 percent to the United States and Canada and 90 percent of the balance, or about 864,00, to Argentina, Brazil and Venezuela.[28] De Avila's estimate of total immigration (not just European) to Brazil from 1946 to 1952 was 260,000.[29] The United Nations' estimate for European immigrants to Argentina for 1947 to 1952 was 607,000.[30] Neiva, using gross overseas migration for the period 1946 to 1960, came up with a gross immigration figure to Latin America of 2,456,000 as follows (in 000's):[31]

Argentina	801	Columbia	238
Brazil	704	Uruguay	70
Venezuela	623	Paraguay	19

While the numbers appear quite high, especially for Venezuela, he notes that re–emigration rates were also high, in particular for Venezuela where the estimated rate was 62 percent for the period 1950 to 1955.

What appears to be clear from the data examined is that the mass migration that was welcomed in Latin America came over-whelmingly from Italy, Portugal and Spain as in the past and flowed predominately to Argentina and Brazil, with Venezuela the only major exception. There were pockets of Germans and other Europeans but they remained relatively small in number, most choosing to go to the United States, Canada, Australia and South Africa.

In the post 1960 period, as noted in the appendix tables, European immigration to Argentina and Brazil declined sharply in numbers, settling at a level that would appear too low to have traceably significant economic effects. The country mixture of these immigrants has followed the same patterns as that of the 1950s, as if the new immigrants were drawn by their contacts with their nationality groups already settled in each country.

Venezuela would appear to be the single major exception. Robbins described it as the "most immigration minded," country in Latin America. With its prosperity resting firmly on oil and an elaborate public works program in the 1970s, its gross immigration was high. "The magnet for Italian and Spanish workers is the possiblity of a quick change in status. Yet for precisely this reason return rates are very high."[32] For example, the European inflow was 84,000 in 1971 and 97,000 in 1972 but the outflow recorded for these years was 85,500 and 99,600 respectively. It would seem that these come closer in definition to "guest workers" than immigrants.[33]

Neiva claims that Latin America lost a golden opportunity for valuable human capital by refusing to resettle the large number of refugees and displaced persons seeking entry right after the war. Of the more than one million persons transferred to other countries by the IRO, less than 100,000 were settled in Latin America. "Neither the government nor the public were anxious to receive these people. This was true mostly to distrust of this type of migrant—until then unknown—and to still prevailing restrictive immigration policies adopted in the 1930s which are nationalistic in approach."[34]

It was to the "voluntary" migrant that Latin American countries turned, mainly for the selective immigration policy they decided upon. Their view of the purpose of such organized immigration sprang from their view of the need "to develop sparsely populated regions favorable to land settlement, to secure a balance between the industrial and agricultural populations, and to raise productivity and standards of living by admitting skilled immigrants."[35]

For this purpose, Argentina allotted a substantial sum of money to establish land settlement centers, reserving part of these for European settlers. Brazil set up similar projects. In Europe the countries of major emigration, unlike previous migrations, gave government assistance to many emigrants, though the self –financing individual migrant remained the main type. Italy, for example, assisted many of its nationals by entering into bilateral agreements with Latin American countries resulting in a substantial minority of its emigrants moving "under controlled emigration schemes that were planned and financially assisted by the government".[36]

Kirk and Huyck estimated that overseas migration drained off about one–eighth of Europe's natural growth for 1946 to 1952[37] and contributed "significantly to the solution of unemployment and underemployment in southern Europe".[38]

With reference to Latin America, there appears to be a consensus that the results of the postwar wave of European immigration were not those stated as the intention of the receiving countries; that the official policy focusing on immigration of farm workers was "unsuccessful both in recruiting such workers and in holding immigrants on the land when they have initially been settled there."[39]

Robbins felt that Latin American countries incorrectly assessed the post–World War II immigration situation by setting policies based on their nineteenth century view of immigrants. These focused on attracting farmers and farm laborers to colonize low density "open spaces," areas which had not been filled in the past by mass immigration because the prevailing economic and social institutions prevented it."[40]

A general agreement in the literature surveyed is that the European emigrant after World War II, (at least the "voluntary" emigrant) was very different from his counterpart in the first mass movement.[41] Kirk and Huyck's description of this "voluntary" emigrant appears to give the greatest insight to the problems they posed for Latin America.[42]

> They were individuals . . . impelled by economic motives . . . to seek their futures abroad. Few of them sought land . . . The typical postwar migrant was neither a farmer nor did he aspire to become one. He rather sought out and often was assisted by his relatives and friends in New York, Toronto, Sydney, Buenos Aires, or São Paulo. Even if he had been a farmer in Italy or Portugal his was an essentially rural–urban migration across the seas. He would indeed be foolish to exchange his status as a poor tenant on an Italian "latifundium," for example, for an even worse fate as a plantation laborer on a Brazilian "fazenda." But this, in principle, is what many countries of immigration would have him do—to settle empty land and to do jobs that natives are reluctant to undertake for sound economic reasons.

Robbins put it more succinctly: "European immigrants today are city–oriented; they do not find compelling the prospect of farm labor in the fringe areas of Latin America."[43]

The conflict of objectives between the Latin American countries and the immigrant appears to be an important factor in both the numbers immigrating to and re–emigrating from Latin America.

Langrod, in evaluating this, concluded that the degree of

success in drawing and holding immigrants appears to be importantly related to the constrictions and rules imposed on an immigrant's freedom of action in order to force conformity to the country's aims. For example, Argentina wanted immigrants for the rural areas, not urban. Rules were set which limited an immigrant's choice of residence, not permitting him (legally) to reside within a given radius of the capital.[44] Since immigrants had some choice of countries, such restrictions may be a factor tending to dry up the immigrant streams or cause re–emigration. Langrod notes that perhaps the "big repatriation movements from Argentina, Brazil and Venezuela may be taken as characteristic [of such restrictions]."[45]

To the extent the conflict of objectives between immigrants and Latin American countries decreased immigration or increased re–emigration, it would have diluted any economic impact resulting from the European flow. However, Latin American countries may well have misread the path of optimal use of immigrants in their economic growth efforts. Thus, the flow of migrants from open spaces to the cities, from farm labor use to commercial, industrial and entrepreneurial pursuits (for which they appear to have had a comparative advantage relative to the native labor force if the evidence below is valid) may have enhanced the industrial process and economic growth.

Evidence on the Economic Impact of Post–World War II European Immigrants

Claims have been made about the evidence of positive economic impacts from the post–World War II European migration. It was found that most claims for such impact have generally been inferred from demographic statistics on migrants or based on assumptions as to their "character and quality" relative to that of the receiving country's population. In evaluating the significance of postwar immigration, Kirk and Huyck compared statistics of males per one hundred females between a receiving country's population and arriving immigrants for a similar annual period. They found, from this sample, that the age composition of overseas immigrants was much younger than the population and it included a higher percentage of workers. They reasonably inferred, therefore, that the immigrant "contributes disproportionately to the labor force in countries of immigration."[46] This disproportionate increase in labor force should also reasonably be expected to increase the receiving country's aggregate income. They also stated the superior human capital case for European immigrants going into less-developed countries: that these immigrants included a larger proportion of skilled workers and professional and managerial persons than the native labor force.

> "In the underdeveloped countries, especially in Latin America, even comparatively small numbers of European immigrants are playing a disproportionately large role in the rapid economic development now occurring in that continent. They bring skills, work habits, and enterprise not commonly available in the less developed countries."[47]

Any direct evidence of immigrant economic contributions tends to be cases of a local nature. Besterman offers cases of the positive effects of immigrants on the area in which they have settled, particularly in situations "where groups of immigrants have lived together in an agricultural settlement, or worked together in the same industrial enterprise."[48] He notes as examples:[49]

1.   The Dutch agricultural settlement in Holambra, Brazil. It was initiated in 1948 with a nucleus of one hundred families. By 1960 it had settled about 12,500 acres and had developed a sister colony with some two thousand people, five hundred of whom were Brazilians. "The influence of this colony is spreading widely. Young farmers have left the original colony to become managers of Brazilian farms, thus they have disseminated the advanced techniques brought from Europe. The settlement itself serves as a demonstration center for local farmers who take advantage of its market and other facilities."

2.   In the 1950s an original group of approximately one hundred-sixty Italian families started the Pedrinhas settlement in Brazil. The civic and administrative center they constructed included (in addition to a church, schools and a hospital), machinery repair shops and agricultural processing facilities. All these, plus a marketing cooperative, serve the local farming population with fifty percent of the cooperative members being local farmers.

In the industrial sector, Besterman noted that the Intergovernmental Committee for European Migration assisted various Latin American countries in obtaining scarce professional skills such as construction, electric power and telecommunication engineers, scientific laboratory technicians and veterinarians. "Many of these skilled immigrants have established private enterprises to meet such diverse local needs as the repair of diesel engines and pumps, the production of surgical instruments and the assembly of television receivers."

Each of these are, of course, a valid example of immigration's economic contribution and they strengthen the evidence on its behalf. However, one hesitates to infer a larger effect from a small and non–random sample. These may simply be reflecting isolated results in narrow sectors of the country.

The limited evidence above compared to that of the first migration wave may, perhaps, reflect its relatively recent nature historically. Its macro effects may not as yet be empirically traceable. It may also reflect the greater difficulty present in seeking to isolate and evaluate such evidence in the more economically complex post–World War II period.

Immigration and Entrepreneurship in Latin America

An alternate case for the economic importance of European immigrants than actual economic evidence has been developed from predominantly non–economic factors. This approach focuses on the underlying cultural values which set a country's social and cultural attitudes in approval or disapproval of behavior essential for Schumpeterian entrepreneurship.[50] Its case is made by tracing the effect these values have on the people who require this entrepreneurial behavior to turn economic development possibilities into realities.[51]

Socialists such as Max Weber have hypothesized that capitalism and industrialization emerged in Western Europe and North America because "Protestant ethical" values fostered and approved behavior conducive to economic development, whereas cultures with other social and religious values have tended to act in a contrary manner.[52]

This intriguing case rests on the testing of two hypotheses:

1. Latin American countries have anti-entrepreneurial cultures.

2. European immigrants were a major source of the entrepreneurship capability that emerged.

The evidence of many studies on Latin America appears to point to an underlying value system that is inherently anti–entrepreneurial, tending to reject as "unbecoming" many of the characteristics essential for being true entrepreneurs as distinct from being a manager. They claim that these values, strongly embedded by centuries of landed ruling elites, set the basis for education and social approval even for the business community.

The sources of these postulated Latin American values were those supposedly prevailing in Spain and Portugal, as practiced during three centuries of colonial rule by the Spanish and Portugese who were born in predominant positions. These "ostentatiously proclaimed their lack of association with manual, productive labor or any kind of vile employment."[53] Instead, land ownership became the basis of prestige and wealth, and the latifundium (large–scale plantation) became "the dominant form of economic, social and political organization. Almost everywhere in Latin America the original upper class was composed of the owners of latifundia, and these set the model of elite behavior to which lesser classes, including the business men of the town, sought to adapt."[54]

It is claimed that these "plantation-type" systems, as in the pre–Civil War South in the United States, tend to develop "aristocratic" values, a "gentlemen complex" among the elite. These lead to elitist values that tend to disdain achievement and hard work, to deal with individuals in terms of their family and background rather than individual abilities and performances, and to look down upon pragmatism and materialism.

A number of studies have suggested the dominance of these values to the middle class. They suggest that the behavior and values of these urbanites reflect their effort to imitate and gain acceptance from the land-based upper classes. Thus many businessmen invest money they made in industry in land ownership for prestige purposes.[55]

Other studies have focused directly on the relationship between these values and entrepreneurial behavior. Martin Lipset summarizes these findings as follows:

"Bureaucratic and competitive norms are comparatively weak. Personal characteristics are valued more than technical or organizational ability."[56]

"Managers are frequently selected on the basis of family links, rather than specialized training" with the entire management group often coming from a single family. The "great majority of managers interviewed either considered this to be an appropriate arrangement under the conditions of their country, or had not thought of alternatives."[57]

". . . a principal concern of the typical entrepreneur is to maintain family prestige; thus, he is reluctant to give up the family –owned and managed type of corporation. Outsiders are distrusted . . . From this evolves an unwillingness to cooperate with others outside of ones's firm, and a defensiveness toward subordinates, as well as toward creditors, distributors, and others . . . Nonfamily, middle-management personnel will often prove untrustworthy and inefficient since they will lack identity with the firm in which the 'road–upward is blocked by family barriers,' and they are given limited responsibility. This fear of dealing with outsiders even extends to reluctance to permit investment in the firm."[58]

To Latin American business leaders "a short–range rather than a long–range orientation to money making is common: make money now 'and then to live happily—that is, idly—ever after.' This means that entrepreneurs frequently prefer a high profit quickly, often by charging a high price to a small market, rather than to maximize long–range profits by seeking to cut costs and prices, which would take more effort."

". . . the overwhelming majority of Latin American businessmen interviewed argued that risk is to be avoided, and that 'when there is risk there will not be investment,' that investment risk is a luxury which only those in wealthy countries can afford."[59]

Thomas Cochran has summed up the impact of these cultural values on entrepreneurial behavior as follows:[60] "Comparatively, the Latin American complex:

1.   sacrifices rigorous economically directed effort, or profit maximization, to family interests;

2.   places social and personal emotional interests ahead of business obligation;

3.   impedes mergers and other changes in ownership desirable for higher levels of technological efficiency and better adjustments to markets;

4.   fosters nepotism to a degree harmful to continuously able top management;

5.   hinders the building up of a supply of competent and cooperative middle managers;

6.   makes managers and workers less amenable to constructive cristicism;

7.   creates barriers of disinterest in the flow of technological communication; and

8.   lessens the urge for expansion and risk-taking."

The basic hypothesis claimed from this evidence is that the entrepreneurial behavior central to economic growth, behavior socially recognized and approved by the dominant culture of the United States, tends to be disapproved in the case of Latin American countries. As such, the economic prerequisites for growth that are natural to the United States would require Latin Americans who are willing to be social "deviants;" or people who are relatively outside of the social system—persons new to the country with different values and strong economic motivation. An immigrant of the post–World War II period might find himself outside of many of the social and prestige restraints imposed on regular citizenry and, thereby, permitted to be freer to engage in entrepreneurial activities.

However, Gilberto Freyre notes that even for those outside the social structure the cost of entrepreneurial success can be high for displaying the traits associated with innovation. It can be strong social disapproval for lacking the "finer moral scruples," and a reputation for being "morally or ethically inferior" by those who are required to follow the traditional conventions.[61]

The hypothesis also claims that efforts to modernize these values and behavior fail because the "extremely prestigious" Latin American intellectuals "continue to reject the values of industrial society which they often identify with the United States."[62] In addition, it is claimed that these landed upper class values with its disdain for "practical work" have remained imbedded in the Latin American education system;[63] that its curriculum emphasis has remained the intellectual cultivation of the mind in such fields as law, political science and social science to prepare the elite as potential political leaders rather than in business, commerce and technical skills.[64]

This view is perhaps best stated by the Brazilian sociologist Florestán Fernandez that the "democratization" of education in Brazil has meant "the spreading throughout Brazilian society the aristocratic school of the past."[65]

The evidence above appears to make a valid case on behalf of the anti–entrepreneurial hypothesis. However, there is a danger, recognized by its proponents, of overstating the case—of viewing these findings in a static context as if these values and their dominance were hard and fast and unchanging over time. Rather, the hypothesis would seem to carry an important insight in *relative* terms, that such a tendency was, and probably is, importantly present in Latin America as compared to the United States or Canada or Western Europe. But one would expect a natural diminishing of such behavioral values under the frictions caused by changing economic realtities: the increase in industry scale and its technological requirements in a competitive world, a rising middle class and its diversification,[66] and even gradually changing patterns of land ownership.[67]

To the extent that traditional values crowd out modern ones in Latin American societies, and entrepreneurial success is not approved as success, there will tend to be a shortage of such leaders from the traditional community, and from those seeking approval and prestige from that community. The national business community would tend to lack what Joseph Schumpeter described as the capacity for innovative leadership, the daring to break through the routine and the traditional.[68] Yet, contrary to what would be expected as a result of the above, considerable economic growth has taken place in a number of these countries since World War II. For example, real GNP has grown as follows (000,000):[69]

	1950	*1960*	*1970*
Argentina (pesos in constant 1960 prices)	7,453.2	10,016.0	15,069.0
Brazil (cruzeiros in 1968 prices)	36,051.0	65,915.0	117,840.0
Venezuela (bolivares in 1968 prices)	11,816.0	25,756.0	46,420.0

It would appear that in the presence of economic opportunities, entrepreneurial leadership did develop. If the first hypothesis is substantially correct, it would have developed from those who were willing to reject the prevailing traditional values, those whom Lipset calls social "deviants" or persons who do not have these traditional values built into their behavior. Thus, someone who is new to the society or relatively outside of the social system, perhaps quite hungry for economic opportunity, would find it to their advantage to enter entrepreneurial activity.

Just as Chinese, Indians and Jews have historically been permitted to fill many of the commercial vacuums existing in countries where native entrepreneurial sense was lacking or frowned upon, so might immigrants, as yet outside the imbedded social structures, feel freer to practice more daring behavior in promising activities. This would seem to be the rational behavior one might expect from the urbanized immigrants from European countries seeking economic betterment and coming from a background where entrepreneurship and business efforts were approved means of success; and where the immigrants invariably brought with them capabilities, drive and perhaps ability to recognize new opportunities superior to those of the native population.

What appears to be reasonable logically may fail when put to the empirical test. If the second hypothesis is not to be rejected, then the empirical evidence should show at least a strong historical pattern of immigrants and their families playing a disproportionate role in Latin American entrepreneurial type enterprises.

The limited empirical studies in this area tend to corroborate this hypothesis. For example, Imaz, in an examination of the backgrounds of 286 "prestigious" entrepreneurs in Argentina, reported that 45.5 percent were foreign born and many of those born in Argentina were first generation, or of relatively recent foreign origin.[70] He noted that only ten percent came from the traditional upper classes and these were mainly concentrated in farm product industries which were extensions of their landed class positions.[71]

In the developed states of Brazil, European immigrants or their recent descendents were important owners of enterprises. In a 1962 random samply survey of São Paulo industrial firms with 100 or more employees, it was found that first generation immigrants owned and directed about 50 percent of the firms sampled. This jumped to 73 percent if second generation immigrants were considered.[72] In Rio Grand do Sul and Santa Catarina, "almost 80 percent of the industrial activities . . . were developed by people of European Immigration extraction."[73]

Even in Peru, where the traditional elite continue to dominate economic life, a recent study concluded that it is the recent immigrants who have played an important part in the newer and risky enterprises producing the new rich of the country.[74]

Of intriguing interest on this subject is the finding of a University of São Paulo study with reference to the type of courses studied. It found that a higher proportion of university students with non–Brazilian backgrounds tended "to take advantage of the new opportunities in occupations which have emerged from the economic development of the city of São Paulo." They tended to study "modern" subjects such as engineering, economics, and pharmacy while "Brazilians" were studying more traditional law and medicine which carry special social prestige. The study noted: "It is easier for a not–completely assimilated adolescent of foreign descent to ignore that prestige than for a 'pure' Brazilian."[75]

In the author's view, a substantial weakness in the empirical evidence found is that most of it was drawn from the pre–World War II Latin American populations and some were based on studies of the entrepreneurial impact of European immigrants in the late nineteenth or early twentieth century. While similar impact might be implied from this historical experience, the author has found little substantive evidence.

A case can be made for the entrepreneurial impact of the second wave of immigrants if one can accept a model of entrepreneurial behavior that includes deterioration over time for original immigrants. This would occur as they sought acceptance and prestige in the prevailing social structure and took on the traditional values, purchasing landed estates and acting in those fashions that would give them social approval. There appears to be evidence and logic for this effect. Such gradual deterioration over time would tend to leave an entrepreneurial vacuum which the new immigrants might readily be willing to fill.

Conclusion

In a study such as this, covering a large and varied region for one complex aspect, one must be modest in the strength of conclusions drawn. The economic impact of immigration is not easily separated from the main body of economic life of a country except in a limited statistical sense. One can, at most, search the literature and statistics available, judgmentally screen the very great abundance and diversity of this evidence and seek a reasonable assessment.[76] In this process there is always the very realistic possibility, as so aptly noted by Spengler, that the effects which appear to flow from immigrants may be due to a variety of other factors.[77]

Subject to the above limitations, the following are the author's views based on the evidence examined:

1.   The post–World War II wave of European immigrants played an important role not only as scarce human capital inputs in the economic development and diversification of certain Latin American countries but, perhaps more critically important, as an entrepreneurial foundation ready to expand into promising economic areas as they saw such opportunities arise in their new country.

2.   With reference to the "anti–entrepreneurial culture" hypothesis, time and the realities of world economic dynamics since World War II would appear to be its natural enemies. Slowly, perhaps, but surely these will undermine values applied to commerce that prove to be inefficient in the international market place.

3.   Latin America should not be expected to be a substantial recipient in any future wave of migration, especially from Europe, both for economic and political reasons. While most of its countries have registered real economic gains, their economies still remain too immature and their wealth too limited to absorb large numbers of migrants under minimum conditions for their care required in the late twentieth century. Only Brazil might have this capability but, given its large and growing population with its high birth rate, it would seem to have problems absorbing its own. In addition, political repression and instability are still the situations in most of these countries with little basis to expect the underlying causes for this to change dramatically in the reasonable future.

4.   European migration to Latin America in relatively small numbers should continue. It will probably follow the current pattern of drawing mainly from southern European countries plus a small but seemingly consistent number from other countries of Europe (see Tables A and B in the Appendix). It will tend to be immigration based on good contacts and information as to economic opportunities for the particular individual. It will tend to take advantage of economic growth rather than be the cause of it, and fluctuate (as may re–emigration) as a function of such opportunities relative to the situations in Europe, the United States and elsewhere (including such factors as political instability). This type of migration, on a consistent basis, should be

mutually beneficial to both parties, satisfying the individuals self-interest while helping the receiving country to diversify and mature its economic structure. Perhaps of more importance, this type of immigration places pressure on the receiving countries to maintain economic and political conditions conducive to the positive flow of Europeans.

NOTES

1.   Richard Robbins, "Myth and Realities of International Migration into Latin America," The Annals of the American Academy, 316 (March 1958) p. 103.

POPULATION OF ARGENTINA AND BRAZIL
BASED UPON NATIONAL POPULATION CENSUS

Year	Argentinian Population	Year	Brazilian Population
1869	1,737,000	1872	10,112,000
1895	3,954,000	1890	14,333,000
1947	15,897,000	1940	41,236,000

SOURCE: Statistical Abstract of Latin America, Vol. 23 (Los Angeles: UCLA Latin American Center Publications, 1948), Table 600, P. 104.

3.   Some substantive source material for this area: Thomas W. Merrick and Douglas H. Graham, Population and Economic Development in Brazil, 1800 to the Present (Baltimore: the John Hopkins University Press, 1979): Arthur H. Neiva, "International Migrations Affecting Latin America," Milbank Memorial Fund Quarterly, 43 (October 1965), Part 2; pp. 119–35.

4.   This list was drawn mainly from ideas suggested by Spengler, from: J.J. Spengler, "Effects Produced in Receiving Countries by Pre-1939 Immigration," in Brinley Thomas (ed.), Economics of International Immigration, 1958, (London: MacMillian and Co., 1958), pp. 17–49.

5.   Of interest here is an estimate made of immigrant effects on population growth, 1840–1970, which found that net immigration togeth-

er with the immigrant's natural increase, contributed 58% of the population growth in Argentina and 19% in Brazil. *Ibid.*, from Table I, p. 26.

6.   Robbins, p. 106.

7.   Eric N. Bakalanoff, *The Shaping of Modern Brazil* (Louisiana State University Press, Baton Rouge, 1969), p. 29.

8.   *Ibid.*, p. 21.

9.   *Ibid.*, Table I, p. 20.

10.   This was a period of rising coffee prices and Brazil produced over one–half of the World's coffee output, most of this from São Paulo. The demand for labor tended to outstrip the supply at the prevailing wage levels coffee planters were prepared to pay. This upsurge in demand also dovetailed with an economic stagnation in Italy, and economic downturns in immigrant competing countries like the United States. Thomas W. Merrick and Douglas H. Graham, p. 96.

11.   Fernando Bastos de Avila, *Economic Impact of Immigration: The Brazilian Immigration Problem.* (The Hague: Martinus Nijhoff, 1954), p. 80.

12.   Merrick and Graham, from Table V–5, p. 96. Inman says: "The general failure to make land accessible in small holdings sufficient to encourage the maintenance and progressive competence of the individual farmer and his family has resulted in the utter absence of an independent agricultural class. . . ." Samuel Guy Inman, *Latin American, Its Place in World Life* (New York: Harcourt, Brace & Co., 1942), p. 133.

13.   Spengler, p. 27.

14.   De Avila, p. 24.

15.   *Ibid.*, p. 61.

16.   Merrick and Graham, p. 110. They found: "In 1900, the foreign –born registered about double the literacy rate (percent) of the native born (43 vs. 23). By 1920, this differential had widened further (52 vs. 23). . . . for 1940, comparative indices in education showed the foreign –born to have had substantially higher educational qualifications," Table V–13, p. 111.

17.   Spengler notes that the southern European who dominated immigration to Argentina and Brazil, "coming largely after the beginning of the great Argentine boom of the 1880s,. . . . though less skilled than emigrants from Britain and Germany, apparantly were as skilled as, and often more skilled than, much of the native–born population." Spengler, p. 37.

18.   Merrick and Graham, pp. 112–113.

19.   *Ibid.*, p. 114. The *colono* labor system was "an unusual combina-

tion of an annual wage, piece–work payments, daily wage, and nonmonetary prerequisites that gave reasonable assurance of a minimum annual income, the reduction of living costs and the possibility of accumulating savings through money income and a low cost of living," (pp. 114–15).

20.   Ibid., Table V–15, p. 113, Merrick and Graham also note that "when one bears in mind that the sons of earlier immigrants must have represented a relevant portion of the native–born owners by the 1930s, the impact of immigrants on the structure of rural property ownership in São Paulo becomes even more significant," (p. 112).

21.   See Merrick and Graham, p. 115, for samples of such studies.

22.   Bakalanoff, p. 31.

23.   Fernando H. Cardoso, "The Industrial Elite" in Seymour Martin Lipset and Aldo Solari (eds.), Elites in Latin America (New York: Oxford University Press, 1967), p. 102.

24.   Dudley Kirk and Earl Huyck, "Overseas Migration from Europe since World War II," American Sociological Review, 19 (August 1954), p. 447.

25.   Robbins, p. 107.

26.   Kirk and Huyck, p. 447. They estimated that at least five million Europeans emigrated but that "return" migration was about one–third of the total.

27.   Ibid., from Table 2A, p. 450.

28.   Robbins, p. 102.

29.   De Avila, "Brazil," in Brinley Thomas (ed.) Economics of International Immigration, p. 186.

30.   United Nations Demographic Yearbook, 1948, 1949/1950, 1951, 1952 and 1954. U.N. Data for this period was not available for Brazil.

31.   Neiva, p. 128. My own estimate using the U.N. Demographic Yearbook from 1947 to 1960 and roughly estimating 1954 and 1955, not recorded, came to 827,000 for Argentina.

32.   Robbins, p. 109.

33.   U.N. Demographic Yearbook, 1977, table 29, pp. 652–54. While the years 1974 to 1975 show no emigration, this would appear to be more a lack of the data than the actual facts, given the consistency of large outflows in the previous years.

34.   Neiva, p. 127.

35.   Witold Langrod "Social Problems of Asorption since 1945," in Brinley Thomas, (ed.), Economics of International Immigration, pp. 304–35.

36.   Kirk and Huyck, p. 449.

37.   *Ibid.*, p. 447.

38.   *Ibid.*, p. 454.

39.   *Ibid.*, p. 454.

40.   See Robbins, p. 103.

41.   In a general evaluation of European emigrants, Langrod found that ". . . there has been a marked change in the character of the migrants. The majority of pre–war and earlier migrants were peasants and un-skilled laborors,. . . . The new migrants have included a high proportion of professionals, intellectuals, and white–collar workers." Langrod, p. 307.

42.   Kirk and Huyck, p. 451.

43.   Robbins, p. 107.

44.   Langrod questions whether such restrictions were effective "in preventing immigrants from . . . moving from rural communities to the cities." Langrod, p. 310.

45.   *Ibid.*, pp. 309–310. He continues: "Migrants of today are more aware of their social and economic rights than their pre–war counter-parts, and migration streams tend to dry up if the legitimate interests of migrants and their families are not sufficiently protected." p. 319.

	1950 Immigration	**1947 Census**
Males per 100 females	147	105
% in age group 20–39	47.6%	32.5%

47.   *Ibid.*, pp. 454–55. One surrogate for judging the comparative human capital differences might be comparison of educationals differ-ences of native and immigrant as was done for pre–war immigrant movements. See Merrick and Graham, Table V–13, p. 111. No such study was found for the post–war immigrant. This, of course, would not capture the more elusive factors such as work habits and entrepreneurial drive.

48.   W.M. Besterman, "Immigration as a means of obtaining needed skills and stimulating economic and social advancement," *International Migration of Developing Countries,* World Population Conference, (1965), p. 197.

49.   *Ibid.*

50.   See Joseph Schumpeter, *The Theory of Economic Development* (New York: Oxford University Press, 1961).

51.   A very thoughtful development of this case for entrepreneurship is to be found in "Values, Education and Entrepreneurship," Lipset and Solari, pp. 3–60. The author has drawn extensively from this study for source material in treating this approach.

52.   Max Weber, *The Protestant Ethic and the Spirit of Capitalism,* (New York: Scribner's, 1935).

53.   Frederick B. Pike, *Chile and the United States, 1880–1962* (Notre Dam: University of Notre Dam Press, 1962).

54.   Lipset, p. 8.

55.   Even in cosmopolitan Argentina, a study indicates: "insofar as the entrepreneurial bourgeoisie moved up in the social scale, they were absorbed by the old upper classes. They lost their dynamic power and without the ability to create a new ideology of their own, they accepted the existing scale of social prestige, the values and system of stratification of the traditional rural sectors. When they could they bought estancias (ranches) not only for economic reasons, but for prestige, and became cattle raisers themselves." Jose Lusi de Imaz, *Los que mandan* (Buenos Aires: Editorial Universitaria de Buenos Aires, 1964), p. 160.

In Brazil, even in the new middle classes in the relatively dynamic and developed southern regions: "Rather than considering themselves a new 'middle class' these newly successful groups have come to share, with the descendants of the old landed gentry, an aristocratic set of ideals and patterns of behavior which they inherited from the nobility of the Brazilian empire. . . . a 'gentlement complex'—a disappraisal of manual labor in every form," Bernard J. Siegel, "Social Structures and Economic change in Brazil," in Simon Kuznets, Wilbur Moore, and Joseph Spengler (eds.) *Economic Growth: Brazil, India, Japan* (Durham: Duke University Press, 1955), pp. 406–11.

56.   Lipset, pp. 13–14.

57.   Albert Lauterback, "Government and Development: Managerial attitudes in Latin America," *Journal of Inter-American Studies,* 7 (1965), pp. 202–203.

58.   Lipset, pp. 13–14. "In Brazil, even the growth of large industries and corporate forms of ownership has not drastically changed the pattern. In many companies the modal pattern seems to involve an adjustment between family control and the rationale demands of running a big business." Where absolutely necessary, family members work with technically trained executives known as "hombres de confianza" (men

who can be trusted), selected more for this quality than their expertise. p. 13.

59.   Ibid., p. 15. He notes that reluctance to take risks may be importantly related to family integrity and a view of the business property much as a family estate. "Where bankruptcy might disgrace one's family, managers will be more cautious than where it is regarded impersonally as expedient corporate strategy." From Paul W. Strassman, "The Industrialist," in John Johnson (ed.), Continuity and Change in Latin America) (Stanford: Stanford University Press, 1964), p. 173.

60.   Thomas C. Cochran, "Cultural Factors in Economic Growth," Journal of Economic History, 20 (1960), pp. 529–530.

61.   Gilberto Freyre, New World in the Tropics: The Culture of Modern Brazil (New York: Vintage Books, 1963), p. 61. He states their actions "are given as an example of the fact that the sons of 'immigrants' are morally inferior to the sons of old Brazilian families as political leaders, businessmen, and industrial pioneers."

62.   Lipset, p. 17.

63.   In studies comparing the achievement motivations of Brazilian and United States students aged nine to twelve, it was reported that "Brazilian boys on the average have lower achievement motivation than their American peers. . . . What is more startling is the finding that the mean score of Brazilian boys in any social class is lower than the motivations score of the Americans. . . . whatever their class may be." (emphasis in the original) Lipset, p. 5, from Bernard Rosen "The Achievement Syndrome and Economic Growth in Brazil," Social Forces, 42 (1964), pp. 345–346.

64.   Ibid., p. 19. He quotes Fillol that when an Argentinian seeks to move up, "he will usually try to do so, not by developing his manual skills or by accomplishing business or industrial feats, but by developing his intellectual skills. He will follow an academic career typically in a field which is not 'directly productive' from an economic point of view—medicine, law, social sciences, etc." Thomás Roberto Fillol, Social Factors in Economic Development: The Argentine Case (Cambridge: M.I.T. Press, 1961), pp. 17–18.

65.   Florestán Fernandez, pp. 196–197.

66.   L.C. Bresser Pereira states with reference to Brazil: "At present, the middle class is probably the social class that is undergoing the greatest internal change.

Three fundamental trends characterize the development of the middle class since the National Revolution: progressive integration of its members into the productive process; rapid growth; and diversification."

From "The Rise of Middle Class and Middle Management in Brazil," *Journal of Inter-American Studies*, 4 (July 1962), p. 317.

SIZE OF AGRICULTURAL HOLDINGS IN BRAZIL 1950–1970 BY AREA (IN HECTARES)

Agricultural Holdings	1950 Area	%	1970 Area	%
to 10	3,025	1.3	9,111	3.1
10 to less than 100	35,563	15.3	60,163	20.5
100 to less than 1,000	75,521	32.5	108,919	37.2
1,000 to less than 10,000	73,093	31.5	80,399	27.4
10,000+	45,009	19.4	34,430	11.8
Totals	232,211	100.0	293,012	100.0

SOURCE: *Statistical Abstract of Latin America*, Vol. 23, table 503, p. 98.

68.   Schumpeter, pp. 74–94.

69.   *World Tables, 1976*, World Bank, pp. 48–49, 60–61, 242–243.

70.   Imaz, p. 136.

71.   *Ibid.*, pp. 138–139.

72.   Merrick and Graham, p. 115. From L. C. Bresser Pereira, *Empresarios e Administradores no Brasil*. São Paulo: Editors Brasiliense, 1974.

73.   Lipset, p. 25. Quote from Charles Wagley, *An Introduction to Brazil* (New York: Columbia University Press, 1963), p. 87. Also see Lipset, footnote 95 for a listing of other sources.

74.   *Ibid.*, study by Francois Bourricaud, *Peru: Une Oligarchie face aux problemes des la mobilization* (unpublished manuscript, 1965), Ch. I, pp. 29–31.

75.   *Ibid.*, pp. 25–26. The quotes were from Bertramm Hutchinson, "A origem sócio–econômica dos estudantes universitários," in Hutchinson (ed.) *Mobilidade e Trabalho* (Rio de Janeiro: Centro Brasileiro

de Pesquisas Educacionals Ministerio de Educacao e Cultura, 1960), p. 145.

76.   The author was limited in this to English language publications, counting on specialists on Latin America for assessing Spanish, Italian, Portugese and German studies dealing with this subject.

77.   Spengler, p. 17.

TABLE A
EUROPEAN IMMIGRANTS INTO ARGENTINA AFTER WORLD WAR II BY NATIONALITY
1947-1973

Country	1947	1948	1949	1950	1951	1952	1953	1954	1955
Austria	41	898	778	604	505	409	283	13	12
Belgium	29	426	255	229	253	230	108		
Bulgaria	17	97	55	50	39	16	30		
Czechoslovakia	165	803	483	199	137	72	36	14	3
Denmark	66	148	151	46	65	51	90	34	58
Finland	2	21	22	3	9	14	5		
France	314	977	829	1,119	1,013	787	614		
Germany*	325	2,249	1,905	2,449	2,488	2,333	2,247	291	264
Greece	220	522	533	422	552	307	222		
Hungary	90	1,823	866	390	241	125	65		
Ireland	2	18	25	15	13	15	19		
Italy	24,955	70,820	97,778	79,833	58,516	39,457	26,794	33,866	18,276
Netherlands	33	130	135	137	154	155	116	191	228
Norway	18	26	65	11	7	18	14		
Poland	2,323	7,271	3,310	839	402	404	286		
Portugal	863	863	970	2,108	2,234	1,694	1,191	818	583
Romania	41	746	286	196	176	180	84		
Spain	7,205	14,720	35,331	42,712	35,300	26,725	14,872	16,445	16,438
Sweden	30	67	24	26	11	18	43	33	49
Switzerland	147	323	305	288	246	248	225	7	7
United Kingdom	137	822	542	285	291	300	281	278	234
Yugoslavia	927	7,414	2,159	633	498	431	412		
Unspecified	35	408	333	56	104	21	9		
Total	37,985	111,592	147,142	132,650	103,254	74,010	48,048	51,990	36,152
Percentage of total: Italy, Portugal and Spain	86.9	77.4	91.1	94.0	93.0	91.7	89.2	98.3	97.6

SOURCES: Tables on International Migration, *U.N. Demographic Yearbook*, 1951, 1954, 1957, 1959 and 1977; years 1954 and 1955 were not available and are rough estimates from table "Emigrants by Country of Intended Residence" in 1957 *Demographic Yearbook*.

*unreported German immigrants may have come in as "unspecified" and account for the jump in that figure from 1959 on.

TABLE A
EUROPEAN IMMIGRANTS INTO ARGENTINA AFTER WORLD WAR II BY NATIONALITY
(CONTINUED)
1947–1973

Country	1956	1957	1958	1959	1960	1961	1962	1963	1964
Austria	45	42	43	43	20	15	24	13	8
Belgium	21	29	11	16	8	38	40	6	28
Bulgaria	10	9	11	15	19	4	5	1	3
Czechoslovakia	14	7	8	17	5	2	4		2
Denmark	18	13	10	29	5	15	6	5	8
Finland		4	2	6	3	1		1	
France	117	169	111	93	86	79	64	52	125
Germany	267	348	230						
Greece	85	209	232	165	48	45	100	47	27
Hungary	33	1,459	202	55	42	19	18	11	8
Ireland	5	7	8	6	5	2	4	1	8
Italy	9,167	14,518	8,503	7,752	4,066	2,631	2,280	1,146	712
Netherlands	31	56	98	118	79	42	27	32	17
Norway	1	4	3	2	3	4	3		5
Poland	31	112	175	189	172	107	106	72	91
Portugal	419	530	764	376	208	384	738	445	215
Romania	17	25	32	71	62	57	12	7	6
Spain	6,037	8,140	7,764	4,720	2,378	4,032	4,560	2,637	1,355
Sweden	6	10	24	16	20	16	9	20	13
Switzerland	37	40	47	46	58	45	46	35	12
United Kingdom	85	137	207	117	111	84	135	62	80
Yugoslavia	201	320	383	348	193	153	161	110	35
Unspecified	1	1	1	158	167	182	114	97	88
Total	16,648	26,189	18,869	14,358	7,753	7,957	8,456	4,800	2,846
Percentage of total: Italy, Portugal and Spain	93.8	88.5	90.3	89.5	85.8	88.6	89.6	88.1	80.2

TABLE A
EUROPEAN IMMIGRANTS INTO ARGENTINA AFTER WORLD WAR II BY NATIONALITY
(CONTINUED)
1947–1973

Country	1965	1966	1967	1968	1969	1970	1971	1972	1973
Austria	16	5	15	13	7	20	24	10	27
Belgium	22	9	3	19	23	29	32	34	15
Bulgaria	1	4	2				4		
Czechoslovakia	5	1	1		18	11	5	3	7
Denmark	9	8	6	3	1	5	9	16	7
Finland		1		4	7	2			9
France	114	44	55	68	99	84	186	120	128
Germany									
Greece	15	30	17	14	24	32	24	10	12
Hungary	7	7	3	3	8	8	6	5	4
Ireland	3	2	2			5	2	4	2
Italy	634	851	761	1,068	1,084	773	594	300	301
Netherlands	34	49	39	31	36	9	26	23	
Norway		1		3	1	6	1	6	7
Poland	138	128	70	35	37	49	39	27	25
Portugal	185	254	195	149	147	99	78	27	22
Romania	22	7	4		3	7	2	2	
Spain	1,037	960	754	806	1,007	978	784	470	283
Sweden	40	20	28	26	36	42	28	31	45
Switzerland	25	43	37	50	48	65	61	91	55
United Kingdom	73	80	88	72	96	100	150	107	75
Yugoslavia	41	35	31	41	30	54	13	17	14
Unspecified	84	111	89	174	170	251	212	140	201
Total	2,505	2,650	2,200	2,579	2,882	2,629	2,280	1,443	1,239
Percentage of total: Italy, Portugal and Spain	74.1	77.9	77.7	78.4	77.7	70.4	63.9	55.2	48.9

TABLE B
EUROPEAN IMMIGRATION INTO BRAZIL AFTER WORLD WAR II BY NATIONALITY 1946–1975

Country	1946	1947	1948	1949	1950	1951	1952	1953	1954
Austria					468	889			
Belgium					542	786			
Bulgaria									
Czechoslovakia					208	441			
Denmark					311	417			
Finland									
France					3,087	3,659			
Germany	174	561	2,308	2,123	4,221	5,241	2,326	2,149	1,952
Greece					146	608			
Hungary					578	575			
Ireland									
Italy	1,059	3,284	4,437	6,352	12,836	12,878	15,254	16,379	13,408
Netherlands					1,407	1,221			
Norway									
Poland					735	758			
Portugal	6,342	8,921	2,751	6,780	19,659	34,615	40,561	30,675	30,062
Romania					207	238			
Spain	203	653	965	2,197*	5,305	11,331	14,082	17,010	11,338
Sweden					593	618			
Switzerland					1,110	1,366			
United Kingdom					2,866	3,106			
Yugoslavia					220	385			
Unspecified*	5,227	5,315	9,764	6,352			12,096	12,106	12,369
Total	13,005	18,734	20,225	23,804	54,499	79,132	84,319	78,319	69,129
Percentage of total: Italy, Portugal and Spain	58.5	68.6	40.3	64.4	69.4	74.3	82.9	81.8	79.3

SOURCES: 1946–1949, 1952–1954 from De Avila, "Brazil", table I, (p. 186); 1950–1951, 1956–1962 from U.N. Demographic Yearbook, 1959 (p. 685) and 1977, table 29 (p. 635 +); 1955 Immigration was not available; total European-born population from U.N. Demographic Yearbook, 1977, table 33 (p. 972)

TABLE B
EUROPEAN IMMIGRATION INTO BRAZIL AFTER WORLD WAR II BY NATIONALITY
(CONTINUED)
1946-1975

Country	1956	1957	1959	1960	1961	1962	1963	1967
Austria	132	120	69	80	56	48		29
Belgium	54	69	63	52	288	289	70	53
Bulgaria			4	4		2		2
Czechoslovakia			5	5	3	1		9
Denmark			46	37	15	24		2
Finland			22	22	9	8		
France	628	805	457	348	325	367	346	189
Germany	844	452	*	*	*	*	*	*
Greece	641	1,220	751	687	725	595	340	33
Hungary	34	2,017	34	18	7	20		11
Ireland			19	16	8	13		
Italy	6,069	7,197	4,233	3,431	2,493	1,900	867	747
Netherlands	356	264	255	325	324	206	231	167
Norway			37	32	25	18		15
Poland	18	124	120	158	78	59		19
Portugal	16,803	19,471	17,345	13,105	15,819	13,713	11,585	3,838
Romania			31	98	198	75	54	1
Spain	7,921	7,680	6,712	7,662	9,813	4,968	2,436	572
Sweden	62	84	72	85	104	102	93	99
Switzerland	171	219	157	180	231	177	126	103
United Kingdom	304	446	431	367	300	335	273	241
Yugoslavia			61	43	20	29		20
Unspecified*		500	895	846	713	662	601	550
Total	34,037	40,668	31,837	27,601	31,554	23,611	17,022	6,700
Percentage of total: Italy, Portugal and Spain	90.5	84.5	89.4	88.9	87.7	87.2	87.5	77.0

Note: De Avila's Brazilian Data Source reported considerably lower immigrant numbers than the U.N. data where the two reported the same year; for example, 1950 and 1951 were reported at 54,499 and 79,132 by the Demographic Yearbook vs. only 35,400 and 62,385 (adjusted for Japanese and Russians) by De Avila. This raises important questions of accuracy. The author used the U.N. data with its greater detail when available.

TABLE B
EUROPEAN IMMIGRATION INTO BRAZIL AFTER WORLD WAR II BY NATIONALITY
(CONTINUED)
1946–1975

Country	1968	1969	1970	1971	1972	1973	1974	1975	Total as of 1970**
Austria	32	22	29	49	29	36	14	121	10,331
Belgium	117	89	104	63	83	36	93	164	
Bulgaria									853
Czechoslovakia	24	10	5	5	2	1		2	2,987
Denmark	55	38	24	14	44	57		79	916
Finland	11	7		2				46	413
France	122	62	71	34	101	72	146	175	9,242
Germany	*	*	*	*	*	404	641	1,248	51,728
Greece	32	3	3	8	10	13	5	32	5,612
Hungary			2		3	1	1	2	10,023
Ireland						13			403
Italy	738	477	357	254	535	402	478	1,356	152,801
Netherlands	163	18	128	69		77	109	239	5,148
Norway	20	27		11		4		21	428
Poland		9	14	36	26	18	10	39	30,280
Portugal	3,917	1,933	1,773	807	1,095	581	426	959	437,983
Romania			1	6		5	7	6	13,971
Spain	743	568	546	281	470	225	244	410	130,122
Sweden	116	15	67	59	69	85		199	1,147
Switzerland	134	19	86	62	91	88	185	325	4,277
United Kingdom	240	171	281	233	301	262	320	536	4,215
Yugoslavia	12	11	25	10	11	10	3	17	11,523
Unspecified*	723	524	535	354	778	11			511
Total	7,199	4,003	4,051	2,356	3,651	2,401	2,682	5,976	884,914
Percentage of total: Italy Portugal and Spain	75.0	74.4	65.9	56.9	57.5	50.3	42.8	46.6	81.5

*most of the "unspecified" from 1958 to 1972 appears to be unreported German immigrants.

**Total European-Born Population as of 1970 Census

CHAPTER 5
MIGRATION TO AUSTRALIA AND NEW ZEALAND
John F. Walker

Introduction

Approximately one–quarter of the earth's surface lies below 10°
latitude south from 50° east longitude (east of Madagascar) to 80°
west longitude (west of the Peruvian coast). In that enormous area
only four bodies of land are capable of supporting several million
people. They are the island continent of Australia, its island state
Tasmania, and the North and South islands of New Zealand. This
area is populated almost exclusively by people whose ancestors
migrated from Europe, particularly the British Isles (including
Ireland), despite the fact that Australia is the land most distant
from Europe of all productive land on the planet. This strange
development of the last two centuries is explained by the fact that
these lands are isolated and most of the land is a bitter, inhospita-

ble desert. Few cultures show much interest in populating distant, inhospitable deserts. The Europeans who developed exploration and geographic curiosity into high arts, managed to discover the usable areas of Australia and the existence of New Zealand. However, European peoples showed no interest in these lands until the middle of the 18th century.

There is no nation with any significant population within 3000 miles of the populated part of Australasia. The closest large population is in Java, Indonesia. The Indonesian government hopes to move some 63 million people eastward from Java up to 1800 miles thus populating Kalimantan (Borneo), Sulawesi (Celebes), and Maluku (the Moluccas).[1] If they succeed it will be the largest migration near the equator in history. However, it will still leave one of Indonesia's largest provinces, Irian Jaya (West New Guinea) virtually empty. Thus, there is no reasonable or effective "Lebensraum" argument toward arable Australia, a further 1500 miles to the southeast.

The British began to colonize Australia by opening a penal colony at Botany Bay in 1788. The early European settlers did not want to go to Australia, but were transported there by the government for crimes against the crown. The government preferred the lower transport cost of penal colonies in America, but had lost them in the American revolution. The first group of ships took more than 8 months to go from England to Australia. This can be compared to the 66 day crossing of the Mayflower 160 years earlier to get an indirect measure of the increase in costs to the British government of shifting their penal colony from America to Australia. Similar differences in costs faced any emigrant from Europe considering an American, as compared to an Australasian, destination.

Government policy has controlled the quantity and composition of the immigrants into Australia for almost every year of its history. Through the 1820s most of the people of Australia were convicts, their descendants and jailers. Rowland observes, "In the 1820s . . . the British government still wished to deter the free movement of settlers to Australia, except for persons with sufficient capital to ensure that they would not become an economic burden."[2] In the 1830s New South Wales pioneered the assisted immigration system whereby an Australian government paid the cost of an immigrant's passage to Australia. During the 19th century all of the Australian colonies adopted this system which was taken over by the national government when it was created in 1901. The assisted immigration system is still in use. About one–half of all immigrants to Australia have been assisted.[3]

In the mid–19th century, gold was discovered in most parts of the English speaking Pacific basin: California in 1849, New South Wales and Victoria in 1951, British Columbia in 1858 and New Zealand in 1861. Following the strikes there were substantial in–migrations to the mining areas. Some of these migrants were from China, particularly three areas in Kwantung province near the city of Canton. Almost all of the migrants were male.

In each region racial strife developed and attempts by the English speakers to exclude, discriminatorily tax or restrict the Chinese quickly developed. Every Australian commentator on this subject makes the point that Australia's early experience with Chinese immigrants was the same as the experience of California, Oregon and British Columbia. It is probably best described by Price.[4]

The economic characteristics of the Chinese were more upsetting to English speakers. They worked hard for low pay. They were good at founding new businesses that the community needed. They paid their bills, saved and invested. Price describes an 1862 California tax on unlicensed Chinese businesses as "designed to make things difficult not only for Chinese in the laundry and restaurant business but also for those moving into textiles, cabinet making, market and poultry farming, domestic service and laboring."[5] In both Australia and California, employers lobbied to fix Chinese or "coolie" wages, lengthen labor contracts and otherwise restrict Chinese opportunities.

All of these acts, by the descendants of Adam Smith against the Chinese, clearly indicates a willingness to use government force to control market entry to benefit themselves. Both the Australians and the Californians tried to keep the Chinese working at low wages in tropical or semi–tropical agriculture. However, small businessmen didn't want Chinese entry and competition in their industries. Nor did laborers want to work for "coolie wages." Up to 1870 there was much ferment, some riots, and many crudely drawn laws restricting Chinese migration to the English–speaking parts of the Pacific basin, but little effective restriction. However, by 1900 such migration was totally prohibited.

The Chinese migrations to Australia and California are nearly perfect examples of resources moving to opportunities. They were a free market response to economic incentives. The same is certainly true of most of the other migrants to the gold fields. Within 30 years the "white" governments made such market responses by Asian people illegal. They also successfully enforced the prohibitions on market behavior.

As noted above, Australia has been principally peopled by

transported convicts and assisted immigrants, i.e., people hired by the government to migrate. Australia and New Zealand have had extraordinarily successful population policies throughout this century. Usually national population policies fail because people do not adjust their birth rates to fit national goals.[6] Australia has successfully passed through a demographic transition. As with other high income countries its population is not reproducing itself. Thus the size and growth of the population are determined by its age structure and migration patterns. Age structure cannot be manipulated very much. However, in some cases migration can. It is through control of migration that Australasian peoples have controlled their population growth.

One of the principal explanations of the success of Australasian population control is the isolation. Table 1 gives the air distance between Melbourne and the nearest large cities in the world. Some distances for New York are given for comparison.

In 1982, 99.5 percent of all arrivals in Australia came by air.[7] Australia has only 18 airports with scheduled airline service.[8] Thus, controlling immigration can be done cheaply and easily. It is estimated that 98 percent of all illegal immigrants are people who arrived legally as visitors but did not leave when their visas expired. The total number of illegal immigrants is believed to be 50,000 or about 0.3 percent of the population.[9]

TABLE 1
AIR DISTANCES

	Jakarta	Singapore	Manila	Bangkok	Hong Kong	Tokyo
Melbourne	3233	3759	3941	4568	4595	5062
	Montreal	Mexico City	Berlin	Moscow	Rio de Janeiro	Honolulu
New York	331	2090	3979	4683	4801	4969

SOURCE: 1983 *World Almanac*, p. 165 and Quantas Airlines.

Auckland in New Zealand is even more isolated than Melbourne and Sydney, its closest large neighbors, about 1500 miles away. Isolated areas such as Australasia can prevent unwanted immigration by individuals rather easily by control of sea and airports. Such areas can also significantly increase immigration, if people want to come, by relaxing the restrictions.

Rationale For Immigration Control

Migration discussions often focus on two questions: why people want to leave where they are and why they choose to go to some specific new place.[10] The other half of the decision is why a nation would want new people and what kind of new people.

The Australasians have discussed these points in great detail. Australia has at different times welcomed new migrants if they:

a.   were from Britain or British types from the Commonwealth and the United States,

b.   were from south Europe,

c.   were from Asia,

d.   were students (temporary migrants),

e.   had skills useful to the Australian economy,

f.   unified a family,

g.   would do "stoop labor," or

h.   none or only some of the above.

When they choose to close or reduce immigration it is cheap and easy because isolation protects them from "wetbacks." When they choose to open immigration they are faced with the dilemma that in a voluntary, unsubsidized, uncoerced choice type of world *very few people have ever chosen to go to Australia.* That problem was solved with an assisted migration program.

Both Australian and New Zealand immigration policies strongly favored white people of the British type in the first half of this century. Much of the public discussion of immigrants and some of the law centered on the economic advantages immigrants bestow on the receiving country. However, the two goals are not necessarily consistent. Pensioners and other dependent groups, even if racially "superior," would not improve the growth of the economy; they might retard it. Strong, educated, hard-working, entrepreneurial but "swarthy" people could have the opposite effect.[11] Nevertheless, darkness of skin or strangeness of voice made one significantly less eligible for migration to Australasia.

Another theme regularly repeated in Australian immigration debates is the need for more people to bolster the defense of Australia against invasion by the "Asiatic hordes." "Populate or Perish" was made popular by "Billy" Hughes, Premier of Australia during World War I, a founding member of the Labor Party and Member of Parliament from 1901 to 1952. The defense argument only makes sense as defense against military conquest. Unorganized hordes wandering the earth to find better places could not get to Australasia. Nor could a low–income society afford to mount such a distant invasion. Only once in modern history has a high–income, well organized Asian military force moved anywhere near Australia.

Nevertheless, in 1944 Prime Minister Curtin recommended a post-war immigration policy to increase Australian population to 25 million. The principal reason given was national security. F.M. Forde, Minister of the Army in 1944 said, "History will one day reveal how close Australia was to being overrun . . . We may not be given another chance. We must be realistic in regard to the necessity for a scientific migration policy."[12]

Although migration to New Zealand increased some after World War II, there was no significant "pro–immigration for defense" argument in New Zealand. Apparently the extra protection of 1500 miles of the Tasman Sea keeps the New Zealanders from the fear of an Asian military invasion that so often colors Australian thought.

Another major pro–immigration argument is the need for more people to improve the output of the economy and enrich both the newcomers and the established population. Extra people can be viewed either as a resource to be used to produce more output or as a liability that consumes more of a given output. As a society swings from a people–are–resources to a people–are–liabilities point of view, their demand for immigrants declines. Any receiving society whose demand for people changes can limit immigration. They need only control their borders. As we have seen, the Australian and New Zealand borders are easily and cheaply controlled by geographic factors.

Surprisingly, New Zealand with a temperate climate, beautiful terrain, an area equal to Japan or Great Britain, a high standard of living, and good public health statistics actually suffered net emigration in the late 1860s, from 1880 to 1991, from 1931 to

1935,[13] and in most years since 1968.[14] Most of her population increase has been explained by native fertility and mortality since the late 1870s.[1516]

With a current total population of 3.2 million, who are substantially descendants of people who migrated over a century ago, New Zealand immigration has no significant effect on the population of other nations. However, New Zealand emigration may become significant in the future development of Australia because of a noticeable trans–Tasman Sea migration which has usually been in favor of Australia in recent years.

The Australian experience is quite different. At the end of World War II, the Australians, after extensive debate, reached a consensus on population goals. Population was to increase 2 percent per year. One percentage point from natural increase, the other from immigration. From 1947 to 1971 the immigration totals were 91 percent of the immigration goals. Then, forces inside Australia began to encourage the government to lower the target, as Australia suffered the general slowdown in economic growth that has affected many industrial countries in the last 15 years. Also, "suitable" migrants became harder to find.

In the post–war period the word "suitable" has been extensively redefined. Australia has accepted people from Southern and Eastern Europe, Latin America and even Asia, a great change over the past.

Until 1947 Australia controlled immigration for military or economic reasons subject to a racial veto. Asians, no matter how skilled or (Australian) patriotic or hard working were unacceptable. Since World War II they have become increasingly acceptable, especially if economically useful.

However, total immigration is still controlled with amazing precision. "In mid–1978 the government announced a triennium net migration target, (1978 to 1981) of 210,000. That is an average of 70,000 or 0.5 percent a year. To offset loss of former settlers and native Australians, this meant a new settler intake of 270,000 or 90,000 a year. In practice this target is being achieved: settler intake (here including persons who arrive as visitors and stay on as settlers) averaged 89,000 or so in the 3 year period 1977 to 1979 and net immigration some 70,400."[17]

Another reason for accepting immigrants into Australia is various forms of humane response to the problems of people in Australia and other parts of the world. This includes: substantial foreign aid in the form of educating foreign, often "racially unacceptable" students; unifying families; accepting some British

Commonwealth responsibilities to assist and shelter the deserving needy; and accepting some of the millions of homeless and stateless refugees created by the wars of this century.

Almost all of these groups and particularly Australian responsibilities to them were debated extensively at various times in this century.[18] However, the changes in policy to expand non-British immigration were not made until after the second World War. The consensus up to 1947 was that Australia should remain not just white but British. Indeed the British proportion of the Australian population increased from 56 percent in 1901 to 71 percent in 1947.[19]

Arthur Calwell, Minister for Immigration (1945-1949) had planned to maintain the "tradition of 10 Britons for every foreigner."[20] However, it was quickly realized Britain could not supply the numbers of people wanted so Australia shifted toward "acceptable" parts of the displaced persons of Europe. That is, humane was also efficient.

Humane became difficult as Australian occupation troops returned with Japanese or Filipino war brides. The Labor government tried to deport the women and the Asian war refugees who had gotten to Australia during the war. The Australian Supreme Court delayed the deportation and the Liberal government elected in 1949 decided to let the refugees and brides stay, although neither group could be shown to be economically useful. An humanitarian act had stood on its own merits. Others would follow.

Variations of the notion of excessive population density and attendant ecological problems were sometimes used by Australasians to defend closing or limiting immigration. In the 1930s, these discussions led to calculations of the "absorption capacity" of the land; in the 1970s it was pollution counts per person or acre.[21]

Australia and New Zealand are among the least densely populated places on earth, even if the enormous low rainfall areas of Australia are not counted in measuring population density or carrying capacity. Such discussions from the earth's empty quarter annoy their Asian partners in the British Commonwealth who calculate the population holding capacity at a much larger number than do Australasians.[22]

The unreality of the arguments by Australasians can be seen in the 1983 *New Zealand Official Yearbook* which observes "an average population density at the 1981 Census of Population of 11.8 persons per square kilometer. This is low by international standards (for example the United Kingdom has 229 persons per square kilometer and the Netherlands 344) but it must be remembered that in New Zealand there is a great deal of high mountainous country, particularly in the South Island, and also large areas of rough hilly country which cannot be closely settled."[23] This view ignores two critical points. First, other mountainous countries are much more densely populated (Switzerland has 152 people per square kilometer). Second, New Zealand is 85 percent urban. Her people use almost none of the available land. Australia is also 85 percent urban.

Techniques of Migration Control

The two principal tools for the governmental control of migration to Australasia are "assisted passage" and a strong socially supported and socially responsive civil service in the immigration department.

Civil Service

The first Australian Parliament debated the exclusion of Asians in enacting the Immigration Act of 1901. It chose to avoid explicitly stating that it was Australian national policy to exclude Asians. However, everyone agreed then and appears to still agree that "whites only" was the policy. To achieve that unstated goal they left great discretion in the hands of immigration control officers.

The principal tool to exclude the unwanted was the dictation test. With minor variations it was the principal exclusion tool of the immigration officers from 1901 to 1958. Its original text is:

> Any person who when asked to do so by an officer fails to write out at dictation and sign in the presence of the officer a passage of fifty words in length in any European language directed by the officer [is a prohibited immigrant].[24]

Since the officer could choose the European language (later any language) to be dictated the officer could also decide whether the person tested was to pass or fail. Few people know all the European languages. The unwritten agreement between Australia and her civil service was to keep all Asians and most non–Britons out. The civil service was a great success at this work. The

Chinese in Australia declined from about 30,000 in 1901 to about 5,000 in 1947.

Immigration officers could apply the test or not at their own discretion. Clearly most Britons immigrating were never subjected to it. At first, immigration officers could order the test within one year after immigration. This was later expanded to three and then five years.

Many nations objected to the Australian policy and many surprisingly inhumane acts were accepted as part of the unwritten goal of "whites only." Most of the 30,000 Chinese in Australia in 1901 were male. The Australians either prohibited or tightly limited the unification of Asian families. At first bringing wives and children to join fathers was denied. After much litigation, visitations of some period (1 to 5 years) were allowed but with a mandated three year gap between each visit. Permanent resident or citizen Australians of Chinese race could never confer permanent resident or citizen status on their children or spouses.[25]

The principal problems encountered from 1901 to 1947 involved merchants, students, and non–white spouses of Australians. Special rules had to be adopted for bona-fide foreign traders of Asian origin who were based in Australia. Long term residence was allowed for the men but not wives and children. Australia attracted many students from Asia to its universities but made sure they left after studies ended. If they married Australian citizens the family was broken up or the Australian emigrated. No circumstances leading to an Australian/non–white marriage were accepted as reasons to let the non–white stay in Australia.[26]

Various pressures by offended governments and attempts to unite families or improve the quality of Chinese restaurants led to many court cases and changes in the letter of the law. However, with one exception no change in policy or practice took place from 1901 to 1947. The one exception was an Australian agreement that Indian families could be united in Australia. The ties of empire were strong but the numbers involved were very small.

Race, to Australians, was a question of national origin only partially connected to skin color, hair type and eye shape. They strongly preferred people of the British Isles. As Social Darwinism became the common currency of public discussion a member of the New South Wales Assembly of Irish ancestry took to referring to the Anglo–Celtic race. References were often made through the first half of this century to the Italian, French and German races.

All these groups were considered inferior. However, there was a pecking order closely connected to the melanin content of the skin. Italians and Greeks were disparaged and avoided wherever possible. Appleyard, in discussing immigration changes after World War II, observed, "We have had to ease the restrictions formerly imposed on Greeks and Italians and others of *swarthy* complexion."[27]

Chinese, Japanese, Indians and other Asians were rarely but occasionally admitted to Australia. "Australia is seen as being closed to Jamaicans."[28] It is difficult to find references to black –African–Negro–Afro–American migration to Australia in this century. When Australians refer to black–white relations they are talking about relations with Aborigines, Maoris or Polynesians. When they permit migration from Africa it is white-skinned English speakers whose families have often lived in Kenya, Rhodesia (Zimbabwe) or South Africa for many generations.

In a series of opinion polls taken from 1947 to 1964 the choice "keep them out" was focused more heavily on Negroes than any other group, as Table 2 indicates.

TABLE 2
PERCENTAGE OF AUSTRALIANS CHOOSING TO "KEEP THEM OUT" IN OPINION POLLS FOR VARIOUS YEARS AND GROUPS

"Them"	1947	1948	1964
United Kingdom	0.9	2	2
Italians	38	45	23
Chinese	26	25	33
Jews	39	58	17
Negroes	68	77	47

SOURCE: H.I. London, *Non–White Immigration and the "White Australia" Policy*, pp. 147–49.

The immigration officers still control who gets into Australia. Australian laws no longer discriminate by race, but blacks are not admitted. The officers are located all over the globe, inspecting and evaluating potential migrants. Only those approved are allowed into Australia.

The Immigration Act of 1901 and its dictation test have been replaced by the Migration Act of 1958. However, control of the process remains in the hands of the civil service.

> In other words the dictation test–exemption certificate mechanism, which for so long characterized the control of non-European immigration, is now transformed into the temporary entry permit procedure. Its effects, for practical purposes are identical; both the old certificate and the new permits are issued at the Minister's discretion; both may be cancelled at the Minister's discretion; and the effect of cancellation in both cases is that the holder becomes a prohibited immigrant.[29]

However, the proportion of Asians in the migrant flow to Australia has continually increased since 1947. Up to World War II, political migration scandals usually involved Asians successfully getting into Australia. This often involved humanitarian questions which were settled in favor of "whites only." Since the war the same sorts of scandals have been settled in favor of the humanitarian goal: family unification, refugee settlement, etc.

As the society's willingness to accept Asians has increased, so too has the proportion of Asians admitted. In 1973 all official barriers to Asians were dropped.[30] Thus, the government, people and the civil service seem to be together on the issue.

Immigration of Asians was not a significant issue in either of the last two Parliamentary elections even though Asians now make up one quarter of the migrants to Australia.

New Zealand also uses a system where admission is controlled at the discretion of the civil service. However, she does not admit any significant number of Asians and never has. As noted above, immigration has been less important than natural growth for New Zealand for over 100 years.

Assisted Passage

Assisted passage, that is the government paying the costs to transport people from the rest of the world to Australia, was first adopted by New South Wales in the 1830s. It has been extensively used by the colonies and their successor nations, Australia and New Zealand, ever since.

It is an excellent planning tool. When either nation decides it needs more people, it goes out into the market and buys those most willing to migrate. Assisted passage is easily tied to more elaborate economic and social goals. If a country wants more mechanics, it can pay more for mechanics and refuse to offer payment to welfare recipients. Thus, assisted immigration can control the quality of migration in both a racial and an economic sense.

In New Zealand, assisted migration was restricted to Britons from the mid–1870s until 1951. From 1951 to 1976 almost all of the non–British assisted refugees were Dutch.[31] As noted above, in recent years New Zealand has lost more migrants than it has attracted.

An interesting post-war development in non–European migration to New Zealand is migration from the Cook Islands. These people, ethnically similar to the Maoris with some speaking a similar language, have moved to New Zealand in some numbers (for New Zealand). They have not integrated well with the white or Maori populations and are mostly employed in lower status jobs.[32]

It seems likely that New Zealand will continue to be a British, white, small population country indefinitely. Few peoples show much interest in migrating there and New Zealand shows little interest in admitting sizable numbers of people of any sort. In determining admissions, New Zealand continues to prefer the British but does admit some people deemed useful from other places and races.

Australia and New Zealand have both shown great shifts in total immigration from one period to another. "Australia has been likened to a boa constrictor, taking huge gulps of immigrants when times are good, or when gold, copper, oil and other minerals are discovered, and then quieting down for digestion during periods of war or recession."[33]

Since a majority of the migrants to Australia are assisted, a decision to increase immigration is a decision to increase public expenditure. It is not clear whether the economic boom precedes the migration or the migration with its attendant spending helps cause the boom. What is clear is that the government controls migration and thus the incremental labor supply.

The process is surprisingly expensive because Australia is so far from its target migrants and because of what is done for them. Migrants are brought to public housing and then helped to find jobs and adjust to the peculiar social conditions of the country. If migration is to be increased, more domestic social workers must be employed. Migrants are screened for suitability before they are assisted. Thus, an increase in immigration implies an increase in the number of immigration officers screening potential migrants.

Between a quarter and a third of all people who migrate to Australia, later migrate out of Australia. This two way street is common to migrations throughout the world. The least loss of immigrants occurs among people who do not have the option of returning home, o.g., political refugees. Over 40 percent of the migrants from the U.S. and Canada from 1947 to 1978 later left Australia.[34]

Thus, Australia must pay for passage, temporary housing, and counselling and help find employment for about 4 people for every 3 she keeps. Her laws currently favor family unification over other criteria for immigration. Consequently, she may attract several migrant dependent parents or children for each worker she gets. As a result, her other stated goal, economic need, may yield to humanitarian goals in the late 20th century, just as economic goals were less important than racial goals in the first half of the century.

In any case, most immigrants to Australia are "assisted," and a sizable fraction of them emigrate without assistance.

Table 3 shows that for most of the post-war period, assisted immigration has provided the bulk of the immigration to Australia. Without assistance Australia would have had a small irregular net migration flow. Since most of her population increase has been from immigration, without the assistance program, Australia would currently have substantially less than the 14,480,000 people estimated in 1980.

TABLE 3
ASSISTED AND UNASSISTED MIGRATION

Years	Total Net Migration	Assisted	Unassisted	Unassisted as % of Total	Unassisted per Year
1947–71	119,145	74,283	44,863	38	1,869
1971–76	204,929	104,788	100,141	49	20,071
1976–78	72,044	17,814	54,230	75	27,115

SOURCE: C.A. Price, "International Migration" in *Population of Australia* (New York: United Nations, 1982), p. 56.

The rise in unassisted immigration from 1971–76 to 1976–80 is associated with a large increase in the proportion of Asians, as indicated in Table 4.

TABLE 4
TOTAL NET AUSTRALIAN IMMIGRATION BY ORIGIN REGION IN PERCENT

	1947-51	1951-61	1961-66	1966-71	1971-76	1976-80
British	38.3	30.8	54.1	52.9	54.1	53.2
North Europe	6.5	23.6	0.8	4.9	—	-0.4
East Europe	38.2	8.5	6.5	13.3	5.1	6.1
South Europe	12.1	33.4	29.4	11.3	2.1	-0.5
West Asia & Egypt	0.4	1.1	2.5	5.7	9.0	8.0
America	0.5	0.6	1.8	3.8	8.8	3.7
Africa*	0.2	0.3	0.8	0.9	1.5	3.1
Total European and Mediterranean Races	96.2	98.3	95.9	92.8	80.6	73.2
Other Asia	3.8	1.7	4.1	7.1	19.3	26.6
Other Pacific	—	—	—	0.1	0.1	0.2

*only people of European race are accepted from Africa

SOURCE: C.A. Price, "International Migration," in Population of Australia (New York: United Nations, 1982), p. 51.

In Table 4, the peoples of Western Asia and Egypt are included in "Total European and Mediterranean Races" because they are primarily Lebanese Christians who have successfully integrated into white American society. Thus, it is assumed they will "fit" in Australia.

Refugee assistance has been an increasingly important part of Australian immigration policy in recent years. Vietnamese, Cambodians, Timorese and Lebanese have all been admitted to the Commonwealth in increasing numbers. Currently, assisted immigration funds are restricted to helping refugees. Most of the work is done in the Bangkok office of the Department of Immigration and Ethnic Affairs, which chooses the Vietnamese to be admitted and possibly assisted.[35]

Table 5 shows that Asians have received proportionately less assistance than people of other areas, even when they become eligible for assistance.

TABLE 5
AUSTRALIAN SETTLER MOVEMENT BY BIRTH
REGION, 1959–82

	Asia	United Kingdom and Ireland	All Other Regions
Assisted Immigrants	95,515	825,650	1,343,576
Unassisted Immigrants	241,469	260,404	1,001,192
Reemigrants	11,783	231,810	384,034
Net Gain	325,201	854,244	1,960,734
Reemigrants as % of Total Immigrants	3.5	21.3	16.4
Assisted Immigrants as % of Total Immigrants	28.3	76.0	57.3

SOURCE: Compiled from *Australian Immigration*, Consolidated Statistics, No. 13, 1982. (Canberra: Australian Government Publishing Service, 1984), pp. 60–63.

Table 5 also shows that the behavior of Asian settlers is significantly different from all other settlers and especially the preferred settlers from the United Kingdom and Ireland. When Australia assists three Englishmen, a fourth comes on his own. When Australia assists one Asian, three more come on their own.

When they arrive, almost all the Asians stay, whereas one–fifth of the Britons return home. Thus, paying passage for one Asian increases population by four, while paying for three British passages increases population by slightly more than three. Passage from Asia is cheaper than passage from Europe. If the goal is population increase, the passage costs are lower to attract Asians.

However, the costs of integrating people like Vietnamese refugees into modern European society like Australia are significant. These include: special migrant center housing for new arrivals, a migrant social welfare service, a telephone interpreter service, a community interpreter and social welfare service, grants to organizations assisting migrants, a comprehensive adult migrant education program, including English language training and ongoing learning opportunities, and special English language classes for children.[36] Much of this is unnecessary for Britons or New Zealanders. Thus, the costs per person achieved are as yet unclear.

An important implication of Table 5 is that as Asians discover Australia is open to them, they migrate there in some numbers, even using their own funds. Thus, it may be true that with open immigration Australia would be peopled by Asians. However, Australia has never adopted open immigration. The 1984 to 1985 intake quota is 74,000,[37] each of whom must be approved by the Department of Immigration and Ethnic Affairs before leaving for Australia.

Until 1981, all migrants were classed into four categories. The use of those categories is shown in Table 6.

TABLE 6
CATEGORY OF SETTLER ARRIVALS

	Percent of Total Arrivals				
Category	**1978**	**1979**	**1980**	**1981**	**1982**
Family Reunion	26.9	25.1	22.6	17.6	18.3
General Eligibility	39.2	28.5	29.7	40.6	48.5
Refugees	12.7	19.6	24.5	19.6	18.5
Special Eligibility	21.2	26.9	23.2	22.1	14.7

SOURCE: *Review of Australia's Demographic Trends*, (Canberra: Australian Government Publishing Service, 1983), p. 6

General eligibility is for applicants expected to contribute to Australian social and economic well-being. Special eligibility is for people moving under the Trans–Tasman Travel Arrangement with New Zealand.

People chosen for their economic usefulness to Australia are part of General eligibility, which over the five years above varied between roughly 30 and 50 percent of total arrivals. Obviously, economic criteria are significant but not dominant in Australia's choice of new settlers.

Since 1982 a new point system for evaluating potential settlers has been adopted. However, refugee and other humanitarian criteria are still a very significant part of the new process. For the 1984 to 1985 fiscal year the government has limited total intake to 74,000, of which refugee and special humanitarian places are set at 16,000.[38] Another new category is "business migrants." They are people who bring substantial capital into Australia when they migrate. For 1984 to 1985 the capital requirement was raised from $A 250,000 to $A 500,000 and the quota was 4,000 business migrants and their families.[39] Refugees usually bring their families later under the family unification quota. Therefore, the refugee numbers imply even more migrants in the future, whereas the business migrants do not.

Today, humanitarian criteria dominate Australian decisions to admit people. From 1901 to 1947, it was the degree of "anglo-celticness." People often pay great prices for intangible benefits. The Australian people, in evaluating migrants, have always worried about the possible changes in their own society if strangers are to be admitted. In recent times, they have worried about the difficulties involved in assimilating people of different races, creeds and languages.

Each case involves costs and benefits just as much as attempts to estimate the education cost and productivity of a new worker and his family. However, the criteria are not amenable to numerical specification and mathematical manipulation. Nevertheless, reading the Australasian literature on the pros and cons of various levels and types of migration convinces me that if any people choose their migrants with a cost-benefit calculus, it is the Australians. They currently believe there are benefits conferred on Australia by allocating significant shares of their limited settler visas to Vietnamese refugees, even though doing so increases the government training and transporting bill per person allocated a visa. They were comfortable breaking up Asian families in Australia until 1947. Now, they are comfortable unifying them. Such attitudes affect a society's evaluation of itself and its neighbors' evaluation of it.

Such decisions carry both real and tangible costs and benefits. Australia seems particularly moved by intangibles. However, societies that respond significantly to calls to "form a more perfect union, establish justice, secure domestic tranquility . . ." or "Liberty, Equality and Fraternity," have led the modern world for a long time.

Conclusions

Australia does not attract large scale migration. The largest migration was from Britain from 1788 to shortly after World War II. That produced a current total population of about 18 million, primarily descendants of migrants. Isolation seems to be the principal barrier to migration to Australasia.

Most of the people who have migrated to Australia had some special non free-market inducement. They were transported convicts, assisted migrants or refugees seeking any safe haven.

Control of migration has been in the hands of the two governments, which are unquestionably democratic. Their criteria for admission have included race, national origin, family unification, defense, ecological population pressures and the usefulness of the migrant's skills to the economy. Only the last is a traditional economic variable. It has usually been considered secondary to the other goals.

The other goals are what economists would call demand factors. As such, they are subject to rapid change, which is what happened to the Australian attitude toward Asians. The Australian system is such that when social preferences change, so too do public policies and their enforcement shortly thereafter.

Much of the discussion of migration and peoples in Australasia is based on perceptions that are inaccurate. Asians are described as both lazy and hard–working. Australians ponder the problem of excess population in the least densely populated region on earth. They discuss the danger of Asian armies overwhelming them with great numbers when the largest Asian army ever to approach Australia was less than one–fifth the size of the Australian army.

Australian governments effectively enforce migration policies based on these contradictions. One must conclude that the populations of Australia and New Zealand will be whatever their governments want them to be. If natural increase fails (as is now the case), then assisted immigration will, through the public budget, produce the numbers wanted.

NOTES

1.   "Indonesian Transmigration," *The Economist,* August 4, 1984, pp. 61–2.

2.   D.T. Rowland, "Population Growth and Distribution," in *Population of Australia.* New York: United Nations, 1982, p. 4.

3.   *Ibid.,* p. 11.

4.   Charles A. Price, *The Great White Walls Are Built.* Canberra: Australian National University Press, 1974, pp. 53–89.

5.   Price, *op. cit.,* p. 64.

6.   Hope T. Eldridge, "Population Policies," in *International Encyclopedia of the Social Sciences,* Vol. 12. New York: Macmillan, 1968, pp. 381–88.

7.   *Australian Immigration.* Canberra: Australian Government Publishing Service, 1984, p. 20.

8.   *Atlas of the World,* 5th ed. Washington, D.C.: National Geographic Society, p. 229; and 1st ed., 1963, p. 145.

9.   *Commonwealth Record,* March 25–31, 1985, p. 378.

10.   *The Determinants and Consequences of Population Trends,* Vol. 1. New York: United Nations, 1973, p. 237.

11.   P.A. Lane, *Immigration and Economics,* in K.W. Thomson and A.D. Trlin, eds., *Immigrants in New Zealand,* Palmerston North: Massey University, 1970, p. 25–37; and R.T. Appleyard, *Immigration and National Development* in Hew Roberts, ed., *Australia's Immigration Policy,* Nedlands: University of Western Australia, 1972, pp. 13–28.

12.   R.T. Appleyard, "Immigration and National Development," in Hew Roberts, ed., *Australia's Immigration Policy,* Nedlands: University of Western Australia Press, p. 16.

13.   E.P. Neale, "Some Statistical Aspects of New Zealand Migra-

tion," in W.G.K. Duncan and C.V. James, eds., *The Future of Immigration*, Sydney: Ausus & Robertson Ltd., 1937, pp. 218–22.

14.   *1983 New Zealand Official Yearbook*, Wellington: Department of Statistics, 1984, p. 101.

15.   Neale, *op. cit.*, p. 217.

16.   Oliver, *op. cit.*, p. 400.

17.   C.A. Price, "International Migration Contributions to Growth and Distribution of Australian Population" in *Population of Australia*, Vol. I, N.Y.: United Nations. 1982. pp. 49–50.

18.   See especially A.C. Palfreeman, *The Administration of the White Australia Policy*. Melbourne: Melbourne University Press, 1967.

19.   Charles Price, "Migration to and from Australia," in T.F. Smith, ed., *Commonwealth Migration*. London: Macmillan, 1981, p. 19.

20.   *Ibid.*, p. 22.

21.   Duncan and James, *The Future of Immigration*. Sydney: Angus & Robertson, Ltd., 1937, pp. 167–216, 241–57.

22.   S. Chandrasekar, *Asia's Population Problems with a Discussion of Population and Immigration in Australia*. New York: Frederick A. Praeger, 1967, pp. 211–276.

23.   *1983 New Zealand Official Yearbook, op. cit.*, p. 73.

24.   Palfreeman, *op. cit.*, p. 81.

25.   *Ibid.*, p. 18.

26.   *Ibid.*, pp. 40–47, 51–58.

27.   Appleyard, *op. cit.*, p. 20.

28.   T.E. Smith, "Emigration from Jamaica," in his *Commonwealth Migration*. London: Macmillan, 1981, p. 169.

29.   Palfreeman, *op. cit.*, p. 109.

30.   W.D. Bovrie, "Overview: Some Reflections," in *Population of Australia*, Vol. 2. New York, United Nations, 1982, p. 555.

31.   G.T. Bloomfield, *New Zealand: A Handbook of Historical Statistics*. Boston: G.K. Hall & Co., 1984, pp. 76–77.

32.   P.H. Curson, "The Cook Islanders," in K.W. Thomson and A.D. Trlin, eds., *Immigrants in New Zealand*, Palmerston North: Massey University, 1970, p. 168–97.

33.   Price, "International Migration," p. 46.

34.   *Ibid.,* p. 53.

35.   *1983 Yearbook of Australia.* Canberra: Australian Bureau of Statistics, 1984, p. 144.

36.   *1983 New South Wales Yearbook,* Australian Bureau of Statistics, S.W. Office, 1984, p. 71–72.

37.   *Commonwealth Record,* August 20–26, 1984, p. 1585.

38.   *Ibid.*

39.   *Commonwealth Record,* July 16–22, 1984, p. 1325.

Notes on Contributors

Sidney Klein, Editor
Professor of Economics, California State University, Fullerton; Distinguished Teaching Award, Western Economics Association (1976); author of numerous books including *The Road Divides: Economic Aspects of Sino-Soviet Rift* (1966), *Applied General Statistics* (3rd ed., 1967), and *Politics Versus Economics: The Foreign Trade and Aid Policies of China* (1968); consultant to public and private agencies.

Paul Kuznets
Professor of Economics, Indiana University; publications include *Economic Growth and Structure in the Republic of Korea* (1977); served as an advisor to the Korea Development Institute; member of Midwest Universities Consortium for International Activities consultative group working in Indonesia with the University of Northern Sumatra.

M.C. Madhavan
Professor of Economics, San Diego State University; Assistant Secretary of the Economic Committee of the World Bank, (1963 to 1968); accompanied World Bank missions to Iraq and Greece; has published extensively in the area of economic development.

Norman Plotkin
Professor of Economics, U.S. Naval Postgraduate School, California (retired); Visiting Professor to the Federal Communication Commission (1980 to 1982).

Edwin P. Reubens
Emeritus Professor of Economics, City College of the City University of New York; policy consultant for UNICEF, U.S.A.I.D., Select Commission on Immigration and Refugee Policy (Hesburgh Commission), the Brookings Institution, and U.S. House of Representatives Subcommittee on Immigration. His latest book is *The Challenge of the New International Economic Order* (1981).

John F. Walker
Professor of Economics, Portland State University; member of editorial board of *The Western Tax Review* and board of directors of the Western Tax Association; has published extensively on the role of government in the economy.

INDEX

≈ DEMCO ≈